Metamorphosis Of A Misfit

Copyright © 2018 by Kirsty H Blattner

All rights reserved. This book or any portion thereof may not be reproduced or used in any manner whatsoever, without the express written permission of the publisher, except for the use of brief quotations in a book review.

Printed in the United States of America

First Printing, 2018

ISBN 9-780692-168912

Kindle Direct Publishing

Graphic Designer: Dino Buljubasic

Back Cover Photo: Ania Fields http://www.aniafieldsphotoart.com/#!/home

-User Guide-

- ☐ To be a phenomenal leader, it's vital to develop SELF leadership.

- ☐ If you're a parent, teacher, coach, CEO, COO, youth leader, elder inspirer, speaker, author, team leader - you're a LEADER. If you lead a group, organization or country - you're a LEADER.

- ☐ To get the most out of this book, use your intuition and turn to a page that you're drawn to. If this sounds absurd to you, use this book logically and scan for a chapter that resonates with you or read it from start to finish.

- ☐ Everyone has bio-individuality, meaning you learn in different ways. If you learn best from reading and contemplating, do that. If you learn best from scribbling in margins, highlighting and journalling, do that. If you learn best by creating or being in a book club, do that. The more you feel, learn, study or contemplate, this book, the more benefit you'll receive from it.

- ☐ Know that some things may resonate with you and some may not, and either way, that's OK. Take in what you need, ignore the rest.

- ☐ Release the need to get immediate results or magically transform yourself in minutes AND hold a space that these things may also be possible and plausible!

- ☐ In order to be a Luminous Legendary Leader, and a Magnificent Misfit Leader that gets extraordinary results, spend time on SELF leadership.

- ☐ Take action when reminded, inspired or encouraged from these pages. Intention, without action, leads to procrastination, frustration and stuck-ness.

- ☐ Find, create or put together a tribe that'll assist you to get to where you want to go. This will allow your journey to be fast tracked and provide you with guidance and accountability.

- ☐ Access and discover ALL the tools and techniques available to you. Remember that small steps, taken consistently, will have massive impacts.

- ☐ Let me know, how I can assist you on your journey. It's my passion and privilege to assist leaders to be their best, to empower, strengthen and provide, tools and techniques to exemplify leadership qualities.

- ☐ You're as unique as you are talented. There are millions of different ways to reach the same result. Find what works best for you, have faith, resilience and support to get to where you want to go.

-Dedication-

To the two loves of my life. My gorgeously amazing husband Cris, who's helped me to become more ME and always embraces my misfit mayhem with pure love and laughter. Our daughter Zennia who's essence reminds me of depths of love, I barely knew existed. Her laughter and spirit motivate me to be the best human I can possibly and impossibly be! Cris and Zen, fill my life with; effervescence, adventures, inspiration, and a love so expansive, It fills every fibre of my being. Without them, this book would not exist and my life, less shiny, magnificent and fantastical.

-Testimonies-

I got the honor of hearing Kirsty Blattner recite one of her poems live. I was mesmerized. Her words are like notes to a beautiful song - each one tapping into the heart of the listener and weaving a tapestry of human life. If you can experience her work, do it. It will be the gift you give yourself.

Kelly Swanson
Motivational Speaker, Author

www.motivationalspeakerkellyswanson.com

Kirsty is one of our all-time favorite humans! Maybe it's her infectious smile, or her kind eyes, or her adventurous spirit. Maybe it's the way she zigs when others zag. Or maybe it's the way she uses poetry to communicate some of life's most important lessons in a way that gets past even the most impenetrable force fields of cynicism. Whatever it is, Kirsty always delivers a fresh defense against Adultitis, and this lovely collection of poems is no exception.

Kim and Jason Kotecki
Founders of the Cure Adultitis Institute

www.EscapeAdulthood.com

Have you ever wondered what it looks and feels like to sparkle as a person? Well, you just need to meet Kirsty! When I first heard Kirsty speak, I laughed, I smiled, I pondered deeply, I let go a little, and I cried. Kirsty's words and voice touched my soul. She has powerful, insightful, provocative questions and insights that push you to go within and find your best self. While her life has not all been rainbows and roses, she finds the beauty and magic of each day and spreads that out into the world. She has the unique capability of instilling inspiration, hope and joy to others. You will find Kirsty's book to be authentic, vulnerable, brave, and magical.

Frances Parker
Wellbeing Lifestyle Coach

www.radiantdailywellbeing.com

Kirsty has a brilliant and beautiful way she articulates her voice. She has a strong, important message in her poems. Metamorphosis of a Misfit definitely hits me home with it's messages and I know it'll make a powerful and impacting read for many others.

Tofe Evans
Resilience Thought Leader | Limit Pusher

Tofe-Evans.com

In one of her poems, Kirsty expresses a wish to be a **bird who could fly.** That is exactly what this book does! It lifts the reader up with its wings and soars us to a higher ground. The format of a giving background, gifting a poem, and offering questions, gives words to the very struggles we all face. She starts us with the struggle, grounds us in her truth, and lifts us up with powerful words and images. Never preachy. Never forced. Always authentic and vulnerable. A book for all of us misfits who want to fly.

Theresa Kim
Founder of the Meditative Creativity Movement

www.suite101experiences.com

Metamorphosis of a Misfit is a refreshing mix of creativity and self-improvement drills, unlike any other book I've ever experienced! *Metamorphosis of a Misfit* is self-reflection in its purest form and encourages you to dig into your soul and understand who you are and why. Kirsty makes practicing awareness, understanding, and gratitude simple by connecting exercises through poetry.

Chantel Soumis
Marketing Sorcerous

www.chantelsoumis.com

Kirsty asks herself the big questions of life. They why am I here, the *what am I supposed to be doing*, the why aren't I good enough questions. As a woman and as a person struggling in a world of perfection, Kirsty shares her personal story and then gives me room to step into the poems, to use her questions to continue my journey. Brilliant book to encourage, enlighten and enrage us to ponder our own metamorphosis.

Mary Helen Conroy
Speaker, Coach, Author

www.lifesadaringadventure.com

What I respect and appreciate most about Kirsty's work is how she leads you from one mind space to another. Moving from creative space to thoughtful reflective space and back. This is an extremely powerful tool for growth and personal development. Her stories are human and resonant. Her poetry has the kind of intimacy that turns annoying coffee shop encounters, into a moment of pure connection.

I highly recommend Metamorphosis of a Misfit, for those who understand with their minds, they are not alone and need help feeling it in their hearts.

Jacy Imilkowski
Speaker, Trainer, Coach

www.jacyimilkowski.com

It doesn't get any more down-to-Earth, practical, and fun than Kirsty Blattner's latest treasure, *Metamorphosis of a Misfit*. Navigating the spiritual development and self-help world can be heavy and confronting, and I love how Kirsty infuses her unique humorous and welcoming approach to make any spiritual obstacle not only feel traversable, but an exciting, grand adventure. I appreciated the breadth and depth of her poems and how I could apply them to many life situations with lightness and ease. Her workbook exercises brought life-changing, enlightening insights into areas I had not previously considered. It is refreshing to read uplifting spiritual material that imparts both wisdom and luminosity to the soul.

Carrie Jain
Mindfulness Educator and Coach

Kirsty Blattner is a treasure. Her global travels and life's experience have enriched her brilliant creative style and profound insights deeply and we are fortunate to now have access to her reflections. Everything she does is with the generosity of a servant's heart and her authentic conviction for helping others is evident in the way she writes, speaks, and lives. It is an honor to join her on her journey through her profound and meaningful poetry.

Susan Young
Positive Impact & Change Expert Speaker, Author

www.SusanCYoung.com

I. STUCK IN THE MUCK

-Stuck-

Stuck Sucks	12 - 19
Nothing & Worse	20 - 25
All Is Not What It Seems	26 - 38

-Tragedy To Triumph-

Poem For Kaimi	40 - 49
Sky Dog's Poem	50 - 62
You Made a Difference To Me	63 - 71

-Grand Grief-

You're A Goddess	73 - 80
I Remember	81 - 86
Best Foreign Friend Forever (BFFF)	87 - 96

-Mom's The Word-

Marjorie & Sage	98 - 105
Momma Bear	106 - 118
I'm Not OK	119 - 128

II. SERINDIPITY

-Kinesthetic-

Run To Me	130 - 137
Finding Your Authentic Self	138 - 147
Power Of Play	148 - 156

-Truths-

Trust The Universe	158 - 164
Trials To Transformation	165 - 173
Recalibration Reals	174 - 182

-Treks Tracks & Travel-

Same Same But Different	184 - 195
Am I There Yet	196 - 205
Rambling Rose	206 - 214

-Introspection-

Versatile Vulnerability	216 - 225
Bio-Individual Bravery	226 - 234
Inner Wisdom	235 - 243

III. SUBLIME

-Tribe-

Kool Kids	245 - 254
Trust & Adjust	255 - 263
What's Possible Now	264 - 273

-Desired State-

Continental Confidence	275 - 284
Stress To Sublime	285 - 297
Piece of Peace	298 - 306

-Magnanimous Love-

Joy Of Zen	308 - 316
Love Of My Life	317 - 328
Zen Fish	329 - 338

-Future Footprints-

Scripting Your Story	340 - 350
Future You	351 - 359
Stop It	360 - 370

-Visualizations-

Childlike Lens	372 - 381
Imagine	382 - 391
Illusion Of Limitations	392 - 400

Author Bio	401

-Stuck-

Stuck Sucks

I clearly remember the MANY moments and years, where I had meltdowns about being an entrepreneur. This time in particular, I was feeling stressed about money, my decision to be a professional speaker, coach and author. As well as dealing with the feeling of isolation. I was a solo-preneur and had not discovered networking! On some level I was willing people, just to show up at my door, the fantasy was that I'd welcome them in and swoosh them off to my office! I really believed that e-mail and website would bring the clients I needed, needless to say this was not working and I was terrified of failing AGAIN! I could see clear patterns of chasing shiny objects, spending money on courses, paying for what I believed would be my next saving grace and then I'd fall flat on my face. I'd feel embarrassed, ashamed, guilty and like I was never doing or having ENOUGH. This pattern would play out in various forms and on this particular day, I was sick to death of its repetitive nature. Then I saw a true reflection of who I was becoming and where I had come from - it was like a weight lifted and the gift of hope had once again saved me from the depths of despair. This was just before I found my coaching tribe, my angel pose, that would save me from myself many times over during the next few years. Until that time, I had limited understanding of the power of tribe and truth. I didn't comprehend the power and trust of one amazing friend to hear my darkest fears and without judgement, pick me up and get me back on my path again. Asking for help was never something I was good at or even knew how to access. I'm a recovering "I'm an island and can do everything all by my independent self" person. Illumination is amazingly powerful and even more beautiful when it arrives through darkness.

Metamorphosis Of A Misfit

Being stuck sucks
making pebbles - not big bucks

Scraping under couch cushions and in the car
needing rent money and hope seeming so far

The same mistakes repeating over again
1,2,3...10!

Having the knowledge and insight with what to do
and still not being able to follow through

The frustration of recognizing the situation like a foe
there you are, I see you and why won't you go?

Why do I repeat the same thing over and again
will I ever learn, to write my story with a pencil - not a pen

It's there, I see it, I know of its destruction
yet there's an unconscious obstruction

I'm sick of being here and of the pain
I think I may be slightly insane

For real, how many people are this ridiculous?
if only everything could be solved with this!

My eyes stinging from my latest disaster
maybe there is no happy ever after

Metamorphosis Of A Misfit

Person by person, book by book, trial and error
I discovered some information that made this mess clearer

I was not broken and in need of fixing
I just needed the right ingredients and to keep on mixing

Mixing an alchemy of life, happiness, money and love
maybe even a turtle dove

Forgiveness, peace, self-awareness and trust
I can feel it now, that lust

Lust for life, love and passion
served up in a healthy ration

My lessons in life are gifts for others tomorrow
like you, I've experienced grief, heartache, pain and sorrow

Now I have the tools, techniques and experience to grow
sometimes it can seem a little slow!

Yet the lights in sight and every day I rekindle the fire
living from my heart and strengthening my desire

My desire to make a living from what I love the most
I can feel the ocean and see our house on the coast

I'm not there yet and the difference is: now I have a path
I don't feel like I'm being torn and ripped in half

Metamorphosis Of A Misfit

Thoughts and gremlin brain will always be with me
now I can face them and don't feel the urge to flee

I'm breathing easy, knowing there's my business
and universe business

Choosing to focus on my realm of abilities
not pawing at everything, jumping around like a jar of fleas

Staying focused on where I can make the greatest difference in life
assisting others and guiding them through their strife

Not living to your true potential sucks
following your heart can have you leaping for joy and create big bucks

So which path will you choose
the one less travelled or the one, you know you'll lose

The choice is yours, stuck can suck
freedom is liberating and brings with it a bounty of luck

Choose your odyssey with passion and heart
feel the energy within you, not apart

Your unique dreams may differ from another
don't let them put your dreams out with a smother

Find a way to live bright, bold and loud
do what it takes to stand tall, be counted and proud

Metamorphosis Of A Misfit

You may not see it in you, I do, like lights brightest beams
I believe you are capable beyond your wildest dreams

If you told me 5 years ago, I'd be here in front of you now
I would've replied, that's not possible, no way, how?

Yet it was, it is and that's the beauty of life
once you believe in yourself, your talent, there's little strife

What will you do with your new life? What will be in print?
what will be your greatest accomplishment?

When I die, what will others remember me by?
I want it to be as a bird who could fly

I want to make a difference to billions and you
so remember, stuck sucks and freedom is like a magical glue

That sets your spirits soaring and heart shining
it's life with a silver lining

The world needs you, to do what you're most passionate about
to wake up each day and shout

For love and laughter
a life of living happily ever after!

Reflection Questions

1. What do you do when feeling stuck?

   _____
   _____
   _____
   _____
   _____
   _____
   _____

2. How do you get unstuck?

   _____
   _____
   _____
   _____
   _____
   _____
   _____

3. If you formed a tribe of you and two or three others, who would they be?

   _____
   _____
   _____
   _____
   _____

4. What do value in a friendship?

_____
_____
_____
_____
_____
_____
_____
_____
_____

5. Ever felt like you are so much more than what your life is reflecting? In what ways?

_____
_____
_____
_____
_____
_____
_____
_____
_____

6. What are your long term dreams?

_____
_____
_____
_____
_____
_____
_____
_____

7. What have you overcome in your past to make you who you are today?

Nothing and Worse

This poem was written one day when I was reflecting on my shadow side. Ruminating about where I had been and where I was headed. Sometimes I get lost in feelings and emotions and it helps me to write poems of my life, to capture the; essence of a stage, phase, or rite of passage. It's so easy to forget where I've been and the progress I've made. I get lost in comparisons and future wants, which depletes my spirit. Reminding myself of my odyssey and my personal progress, no matter how small, brings me back to the powerful now. I have so much to be grateful for. The more I search for blessings, the more I find. Life is not about being in a constant state of happy, it's about finding tools and techniques allowing you to flow through states. By sharing my truth, my desire is that it'll allow you to feel fully into yours and know you're not alone. Feeling like you're less than perfect, alienated, strange or a misfit can be isolating and depressing. Knowing there is a tribe that will accept you for who you are, honor your choices and love you up, is uplifting and necessary for navigating life! A friend of mine told me once that she reminds herself that she could be the juiciest, most deliciously perfect peach, and not everyone likes peaches! The road to truth and tribe can be a curiously crazy journey and together we'll make it as memorable as possible!

Metamorphosis Of A Misfit

Ever feel like you were nothing and worse?
I have, so often, it felt like a curse!

I've been down so far that I couldn't see a way out
well I could, it would've been permanent without a doubt

I've been stuck so much that tears stung my eyes
my heart ached, I didn't know how to break dysfunctional ties

I felt like I was nothing, worthless
now I've changed and feel priceless

I've shifted from feeling broken and torn
to feeling immense love and preciously worn

I feel bright and shiny
no more playing small or tiny

I'm living big and building my dreams
To make this shift I've created several teams

Support crews, angel posses, family and friends
I've figured out ways to make amends

To myself and others
and let go of dysfunctional lovers

I married the man of my dreams
my life is brilliant or so it seems

Metamorphosis Of A Misfit

It's a work in progress, you may say
it's a shift that gets closer every day

Closer to my authenticity and passion
A life of abundance vs needing to ration

Having a mindset of not enough and limitation
now I see life as a sensation

There's abundance enough for every soul
helping others get what they want, is my goal

Reflection Questions

1. What's your story?

_____
_____
_____
_____
_____
_____
_____
_____

2. Where has your path taken you?

_____
_____
_____
_____
_____
_____
_____
_____

3. What are some of your greatest achievements?

_____
_____
_____
_____
_____
_____
_____
_____

4. Who do you admire, look up to and why?

   _____
   _____
   _____
   _____
   _____
   _____
   _____
   _____

5. When you feel in a place of darkness and despair, who and what assists you to get back to a place of light?

   _____
   _____
   _____
   _____
   _____
   _____
   _____
   _____

6. Who have you assisted and bought a ray of sunshine to, in your life?

   _____
   _____
   _____
   _____
   _____
   _____
   _____

7. Who is the one person you can count on who will support and encourage you without judgement when you need it the most?

___

All Is Not What It Seems

I remember writing this poem when I was feeling depleted, frustrated and scared financially. The fear was ego based not reality based. My husband has a full time job and we live an awesome life. My frustration was with my desire to have a thriving business, doing what I love, being an inspiration to my family and loving life! The reality was that I was teaching others how to do this and not embracing it myself. I was feeling like the world owed me and wasn't paying up! I was struggling with the marketing side of making my business work and getting close to burnout. I think mainly I was struggling with balance in my life. Where to focus my energy, how much money to invest in what areas, to allow my business to flourish and how much time and energy to spend away from my family. People around me were well meaning when they asked me how I was doing. I assumed they didn't really want to know, so told them some vague line and probably used the word fine! I also assumed that people saw me in a certain way and that for me to be anything other, would cause a disruption and isolation. I put so much pressure on myself, I lost sight of what was most important. I was attempting to out run life and my legs were about to turn to jelly. Even a cancer diagnosis wasn't enough to remind me to 'smell the roses!' Overdrive, an all or nothing approach is still something I struggle with! Perfectionistic tendencies and a precious ego, sometimes make me laugh at my own absurdity, other times, I take them so seriously they're debilitating.

Metamorphosis Of A Misfit

Please help me I need the support
I feel stuck like I'm caught

My life is spiraling
feel like I'm un-wiring

Finances are the cause
my need for gauze

To stop the flow
of life being so-so

This is a reoccurring pattern
causing me to flatten

It's so familiar and true
it's not new

Tears sting my eyes
I feel demise

I sob out of control
there is no way to console

I've lost directions my true North
I've lost my self worth

My friend told me the other day
you ask "what did he say?"

Metamorphosis Of A Misfit

He said "I can't afford the luxury to dream"
if only he heard my heart scream

I thought we were a team
what is this crazy meme?

I try to find a Silver-lining
instead of internally dying

I see clouds in my eye
I don't even want to try

I look at my baby
and think one day maybe

She'll have a life I never had
a better one that won't make her mad

She'll learn to trust in her dreams
she'll understand that it takes teams

To achieve the goals
you need intimate souls

This journey in life can be hard
it takes more than a Hallmark card

I wish I had wisdom to give her
I wish I could make it so she'll never suffer

Metamorphosis Of A Misfit

I'm drawing a blank
feel like my boat sank

I feel deflated
intimidated

I can't see which way is up or down
my face a permanent frown

My brain, heart and soul ache
I don't know how much more I can take

The dreaming and trying, feeling the stress
everything is such a mess

I feel embarrassed to tell my truth
seems so uncouth

I thought I had this under control
I thought I could just roll

With the highs and lows
what did I know

I'm supposed to be a coach
feel more like a cockroach

Feel creepy and dark
like what I thought was my mark

Metamorphosis Of A Misfit

Was nothing but a shadow of a dream
all is not what it may seem

People make assumptions about me
what do they really see?

The shattered layers of dreams unrealized?
paralyzing fear of a life idealized?

I thought I had this
not even the sweetest kiss

Can fix this dilemma
can't remember

Feeling this defeated
unseated

Frustrating being so close to making it work
now I feel like a jerk

For putting my family at risk
for taking a whisk

Mixing everything so hard
like a screwed up family Christmas card

On the surface everyone's happy
the reality, it's way more crappy

Metamorphosis Of A Misfit

So many layers, so much pain
insane in the membrane

I keep pretending this can work out
I want to scream, I want to shout

I also don't want to look crazy
I wipe my eyes, feeling hazy

I pretend I'm functioning and fun
I go out in the sun

Hoping some sort of magic will occur
my whole life's a blur

Such a disconnect between reality and hope
don't know how to cope

I teach this sh*^, you think I could work it out
instead, I pity and pout

Feel sad and sorry
for all the worry

I've caused everyone
pressure is a ton

What've I done
to feel so jaded, want to run

Metamorphosis Of A Misfit

Away from everything
to never sing

My life song
it's gone

So tired and worn
want to be reborn

In a different life
without the strife

What would that look like
probably a shiny new bike

Would it really solve my troubles?
putting everything in cartoon bubbles?

Of an idealized outline
one that's not real but a set made from pine

Everything seems so absurd
I wish like a bird. . .

I could fly away
no more today

Have a supportive tribe
with a positive vibe

Metamorphosis Of A Misfit

One with money flowing freely
I believe truly and really

That my gifts and talents were worth the struggle
want to rest and playfully snuggle

I can't talk my way out of this one
it's done

There's no more energy left inside
I cried and cried and cried and cried

I'm tired, been down this path and it's taking it's toll
I no longer know which way to go

Can't sleep at night
wake up in fright

So I ask for divine guidance in prayer
I don't know what else to do, in my despair

The conversation happened although tough
it was simply enough!

To give me hope and encouragement
restore my spirit and heaven sent

It seemed in an instant I went from despair
to colorful flair!

Metamorphosis Of A Misfit

You may not believe and that's ok
the very same day

I received a client as I pleaded
this was what I desperately needed

To restore my faith, spirit and mind
what a gift to find

In the nick of time
so sublime

Although sleep deprived, stressed and on edge
this is what I pledge

To take a breather
make life easier

Rest & relax
chillax

Remember to stay the course
to dream of 'Fantasy Horse'

I'm driven for a reason
no matter the season

I'll always help others in need
I'll plant the seed

Metamorphosis Of A Misfit

Of hope & acceptance for all
no matter if they're tiny or tall. . .

Different colored, LBGTQ
this is what I see and do. . .

There are threads that unite us, you and me
the same threads will set us free

Thank you universe
for lifting my curse

Thanks for the sunshine beams
thanks for my tribe & teams

Thanks for the strength I didn't believe, I possessed
thanks for buried emotions becoming readdressed

All is not what it seems
it's much better by reams!

Reflection Questions

1. Ever been to Crazy Town? What triggers you to have mental meltdown?

   _____
   _____
   _____
   _____
   _____
   _____
   _____
   _____

2. Who in your life is a rational being that assists you from getting mixed up in believing your Gremlin Brain vs reality?

   _____
   _____
   _____
   _____
   _____
   _____
   _____
   _____

3. Where is your happy place? A place you can go and get recharged, relaxed and or inspired?

   _____
   _____
   _____
   _____
   _____

4. What activities assist you to be grounded?

5. What let's you know when you need to seek support and assistance? This may be in the form of a friend, therapist, life coach, healer, psychic or whatever works for you. The important thing is that you reach out when you need to and get back on track to be the most awesome version of you possible?

6. When you're feeling balanced, inspired and motivated, what else shifts in your life?

7. If you had a word, saying, phrase or picture to show yourself when you get derailed, (reminding yourself of your best self), what would it be? How would this item remind you of what's really important in your life?

-Tragedy To Triumph-

Poem For Kaimi

This poem is self explanatory. After I wrote it and gave it to Kaimi, I asked him, if it would be ok for me to share it in this book. I told him that I really wanted to include it, as suicide is such an important topic to discuss and find solutions to get rid of the shame and increase the support around mental health. I told Kaimi that I could take his name out of the poem if that made him more comfortable.

Kaimi is a force of nature and I know that great things are in his future. He has the potential to inspire others and install in them a sense of belonging and worth. He's a natural athlete and one of the best 12 year old humans I've ever met. He may not realize now how awesome he is and I know one day he'll find the right niche and soar like an eagle. His parents and two brothers are amazingly awesome too and as a family unit they are unstoppable. We are blessed to have this Family in our lives!

Metamorphosis Of A Misfit

Kaimi this poem's for you
it's all I can do

From falling apart at the thought of your pain
your amazing human-ness feeling insane

The insanity, is not in you, it's the universe
in that we cannot verse

Openly and honestly about how we feel
about what ails us or conditions of a deal

We all make a deal with life along the way
we have limits and when they're reached, what more can I say?

I don't claim to know you or your experience alone
I can only speak of my own

When I was 13, I wanted to end my life
I felt too much strife

I told a lie
and the result, I wanted to die

Well not die so much as STOP the pain
I felt my brain going insane

The hurt, the guilt the feeling of utter despair
I didn't want to go anywhere

Metamorphosis Of A Misfit

I never wanted to show my face
didn't want part of the human race

I wanted out, to stop the hurt and feel free
I felt tired, exhausted, didn't want to be. . .

A disappointment, waste of space and a terrible child
I knew in my heart, I was wild

This behavior and attitude would not stand in my family
I wanted out desperately

Keep in mind this was 1988
I barely knew my fate

As this moment passed as some moments do
I assumed everyone felt suicidal at some point too

Turns out this is not the truth
I wish I had a magic telephone booth

I'd go back in time and speak to the younger me
I'd let her know that she WAS indeed free

For some things we can't see
they emerge specifically

At the right time, for the right reason
maybe it's fate, maybe a season

Metamorphosis Of A Misfit

I would whisper in her ear
it's ok to feel fear

I'd tell her, her emotional self is fine
in time it would develop into the divine. . .

Work, I now do with other folk
hindsight is a fine thing and sort of a joke

I wish it wasn't so hard to see
the difference you make to me

You probably have no idea that the card you wrote me
when I had cancer will always be

In my heart
it sets you apart

The way you are, your kind nature and being
that's your gift, you're all seeing

You notice what others do not
that's not the only gifts you've got. . .

For you my friend were blessed with many unseen
your essence is calm, still and serene

You wrote in my note that you were happy my burden was gone
your words resinated like a song

Metamorphosis Of A Misfit

You said you can't wait to see me again, this made me cry
as it's so easy to feel alone, even when people are near by

You said you loved me and this warmed my heart
for I knew that your love was pure and set apart

A love that is deep like the ocean
as far as the eye can see

This is why I have a tear streaked face now
because I'm not sure how

To even begin to share with you the love that surrounds you
I don't know how to reach out in a way that is true

True and meaningful right now
so this is how

I deal with life
I write in verse and it relieves my strife

I wonder if magically, my message will transport to you in a way I can't write
kind of like an intuitive insight

I'm not sure if that's possible and I pray it is
I want to say so much and I guess it comes down to this

You are more than you believe you are
you are a shining star

Metamorphosis Of A Misfit

You are more capable than you know
soon, this will show

You have gifts, many will never posses and some are perplex
you choose your path, the steps you'll take next

There is no 'one way' in life's song
you're an explorer and get to experience right and wrong

You get to adventure through left and right
you get to be all seeing or lose your sight

You can listen and hear
or steer

In another direction that calls to your soul
to discover your end goal

I'm still figuring out my place in life
sometimes I'm ecstatic, other times in strife

One thing I know, is following my passion is key
that's the place I want to be

Although not always easy
and it may sound cheesy

I choose to follow my heart
I guess, that's what sets me apart

So my dear friend, I really want to hug you and say it's ok
to remind you, of the love and that tomorrow's a new day

I love you and can't wait to see you again
until then

Dream up wonders and mythical adventures and impossibilities
for in between reality and fiction, is a fantastical set of keys

What will they open and will they set you free?
well . . .that's for you to experience and see!

Reflection Questions

1. Have you or someone you know, ever contemplated, committed or attempted suicide?

   _____
   _____
   _____
   _____
   _____
   _____
   _____
   _____

2. What experiences in your life have been the toughest?

   _____
   _____
   _____
   _____
   _____
   _____
   _____
   _____

3. What support is there where you live, for mental health concerns? What books, people, tools and techniques have inspired, assisted you on your life's journey?

   _____
   _____
   _____
   _____
   _____

4. Who do you consider a role model? What are the characteristics they have, that you admire most?

_____
_____
_____
_____
_____
_____
_____
_____

5. How do you know, when you are not coping? What things change in you your body and your mind? How does this affect your life?

_____
_____
_____
_____
_____
_____
_____
_____

6. When you visualize your ideal self 5 years from now, how do you feel? What do you see within yourself and your surroundings? What are you wearing? What location are you in? What are you doing in your life?

_____
_____
_____

_____
_____
_____
_____
_____

7. If money and other barriers were removed, what would your ultimate dream be? I mean the biggest, most elaborate, phenomenal unrealistic fantasy life you can conjure up. Who is involved with your dream life and how does it feel to be in that place of doing what you were born to do? Who will benefit most from you living your best life?

_____
_____
_____
_____
_____
_____
_____
_____
_____
_____
_____
_____
_____
_____
_____
_____
_____
_____
_____

Sky Dog's Poem

This was written when our Sky Dog had a near fatal injury. It was an awful period in our lives and one we will always remember. We love our Sky Dog deeply and everyday we see him running, leaping and prancing around, is such a blessing. People have told us we're great people for rescuing a dog and saving his life. They don't understand all that he's given us, the joy he brings us every day. His companionship, sweet nature and loving spirit, add to our life more than we could ever do for him.

Metamorphosis Of A Misfit

June 9th 2015, my humans and I
were enjoying a delicious lunch outside and why. . .

Were we all so happy?
my previous life was super crappy!

Today there were hammock rides, my sweet puppy eyes causing food to fly my way
belly rubs, the 'treats game' and this was the day!

My parents had been taking me to dog training school
they were both convinced, I was no fool

I was getting better at recall
I did this pretty well for delicious treats or to play with a ball

Today was the day they wanted to put my skills to the test
to see if I could come when called and the rest

Of the tricks I'd learned so well
time was about to tell

It made them so happy and proud
how could I refuse this wonderful crowd?

Half way to the back door
I had the urge to run off in the opposite direction to seek more

Fun and adventures
to chase the wind and playful creatures

Metamorphosis Of A Misfit

I was free, the wind in my ears and loving life!
My humans came running after me in strife

They caught me on the other side of the road
I thought they must love this game in their excitable mode

Half way across the road to home
I slipped my bandana - my next memory is chrome

I (Sky's Mom) can tell you what happened next from my point of view
I came out of the house with Sky's lead rope new

I looked left to where Sky had run
and my heart broke instantly - no more sun

My view went dark
as I ran toward the bark

My broken baby dog on the road writhing in pain
I screamed NO - NOO - NOOOOOO like a person insane

As if my cries would take back Sky Dog's race
Tears were streaming down my face

I tried to comfort our dog, who's body was contorted
I was sure he would die of pain and shock, being so distorted

Cris took charge and asked me to get the car
we used the mat in the back to scoop up our twisted dog and take him far

Metamorphosis Of A Misfit

Actually it was less than 5 minutes away
yet seemed to take a 24 hour day

I did my best to keep him still and trying
as we sped to our local vet, to keep him from dying

Cris ran to see if they would take him in
we had no idea, what to do in this situation

Bless their hearts, they let us stay with him
they gave us things to do to help (despite his chances slim)

Hold this, place this tube near his nose
We were smeared with blood, I had bare arms and toes

We were in shock, scared our fur baby would die
Cris had some pretty deep pain bites from scared Sky

It was around 2:00
when we arrived at the ICU

8pm when we left
feeling bereft

Sky had 'Poly Traumatic' injuries
no matter how many magical keys

The vets may never unlock all his trauma
It would be hard to tell if Sky would ever recover

Metamorphosis Of A Misfit

His injuries were extensive you see
we needed to make a decision instantly

To perform surgery they estimated $10 000 to work on Sky
we had to pay half before leaving - this seemed high!

In order to save our sweet dogs life
we faced some strife

We didn't have that kind of cash
Cris made an instant decision that we would take a bash

Do our best to save our sweet peanut
do what it takes - despite our financial rut

One of the many reasons I love this awesome man
I saw despair - he saw 'we can'

There were ups and downs and lots of fuss
it took 13 days to get our baby Sky Dog back to us

As grateful as we were to have him back
he was a LOT of work and a heavy pack!

Sky Dog needed 24/7 care - the best
the first night home I received 2 hours rest

The next few days were filled with constant wash piles
sleep deprivation, PTSD from witnessing Sky's trauma and miles

Metamorphosis Of A Misfit

Away from our sweet Sky's usual personality
the shock of a near fatality

Every noise or sound - I was convinced Sky Dog was in pain
we'd have flash backs to the event that were paralyzingly insane

Five weeks later I still have this feeling
although to a much lesser extent, still reeling

I was paranoid that he would wriggle himself to an injury
I checked his breathing constantly

From all the restraints he now had in his life
even going to the toilet caused huge strife

We did our best to make him feel loved and cared for
he needed physical therapy 3 times a day or more

Massage was to assist with his edema (swelling)
and get his legs moving again without silent yelling

You could see on his face and a flinch on his shaved fur
that he was not yet ready for the whir

Of a normal dog day
what can I say. . .

55 pounds of fur and loves was no light weight
I was so scared of hurting my canine mate

Metamorphosis Of A Misfit

When he yelped, it made me cry and paranoid to move him
as a life coach, I knew I was reaching my brim

I knew I needed self care and assistance
I was unable to reach out, I had resistance

To asking for help when I needed it most
thought I could just coast

Through this troubling time
and come out the other side sublime

I was wrong
this event hit me like a gong!

I thank each one of you that reached out, in person or on-line
it really helped me, see glimpses of fine

It really meant the world to me
there were some days when Face Book messages set me free

Reading the wishes, prayers and healing energies for Sky
an unexpected road - frequent lows and an occasional high

5 weeks - Sky is walking, he's wobbly on his new titanium forks
it looks like he's come from Monty Python's Ministry of Funny Walks

With two smashed legs, pelvis and a blood infection
he's now our Robo-Dog of the finest selection

Metamorphosis Of A Misfit

Of titanium parts
who we parade around the neighborhood in yellow carts

We're told - they don't get many dogs that survive
what Sky Dog did - let alone thrive

He had some ground breaking surgery done
vets working on him for 2 days - not anyone's idea of fun

He had 4 surgeries in 2 days without much rest
his poor body and spirit was certainly put to the test

We visited him once or twice a day
and would do anything to play

With our war torn canine
it was a hard line

To stay positive when our hearts were breaking
to see his limbs shaved and shaking

He would only drink water when we put it in our hand
he could barely lift his head - yet was in high demand

Vets and techs fell in love with our rescue husky, boarder collie cross
he was so crushed and also a BOSS!

His spirit and nature shone through
despite his injuries everyone knew

Metamorphosis Of A Misfit

This dog was extraordinarily resilient and sweet
he had what it took to walk on his feet

Although his bill was double
the 10 K quoted and we had trouble

Figuring out how to pay
we would have made the same decision any-day

It's now three years later and there's a new addition
a human baby added to our family collection!

Sky Dog loves her and she him
it's heart melting to see them

Zen giving Sky kisses and hugs
laying snuggled together on rugs

Sky Dog can run, jump and howl up a storm
he's in the finest form

His recovery is beyond our expectations
and brings so many sensations

He doesn't have any hangups about trauma in life
from a kill shelter in Alabama to heart-worm strife

We couldn't adopt him for 6 months till his treatment was done
as the doses he needed were brutal and he couldn't run

Metamorphosis Of A Misfit

As it would raise his heart rate too high
and cause him to die

He was labeled as vicious or mean in some way
no one would foster him to make his day

Those who've met this sweet piece of fur
know he's more like a sleepy cat than a menacing blur!

Sky Dog's sleeping next to me as I write
we're so happy he survived this fight

We love our Sky Dog and always will
he's taught us to enjoy life and CHILL!

Metamorphosis Of A Misfit

Reflection Questions

1. Have you ever had a pet in your life that you loved dearly? What is/was their name?

   _____
   _____
   _____
   _____
   _____
   _____
   _____

2. What was it that your pet/s did, that made them special to you?

   _____
   _____
   _____
   _____
   _____
   _____
   _____

3. When you think about therapy animals - healing peoples spirits and bringing them comfort - what do you think it is that's so powerful?

   _____
   _____
   _____
   _____
   _____
   _____
   _____

4. What brings healing to you? This may be a certain animal, a substance, person place or variety of other things!

_____
_____
_____
_____
_____
_____
_____
_____

5. How do you know healing has occurred? How do you define, feeling better or having your spirits raised?

_____
_____
_____
_____
_____
_____
_____
_____

6. Think of something you would like to do or have that is currently financially unattainable. If that thing or service was of paramount importance (life or death) how would you get the funds for it?

_____
_____
_____
_____

_____
_____
_____
_____
_____

7. Sometimes when we reframe how something is possible, alternate possibilities arise? It's easy to get into a pattern of believing you can't have or do something. What's possible in your life when you recalibrate your mindset, and ask your self 'how can I create new opportunities to make _____POSSIBLE?'

You Made A Difference To Me

This is another poem that I took a lot of time rehearsing so I could present it during my presentations without breaking down! It's very dear to my heart and self explanatory. It's amazing the influence someone can have on your life and they may not even be aware of it. I love it when people write to me or come and chat with me after a presentation and let me know how I made them feel. It's so heartwarming and inspirational.

Being a natural introvert, I tend to hide away and not come out often. It's knowing I may make a difference, that one person may change or be inspired, that motivates me to push passed my ego and present, not for me, for someone who may need to hear the message I'm sharing. I have this happen myself, when I hear a speaker, it's just, one line, one word, one image or exercise and I know, it's exactly what I needed in that moment. What a gift we ALL have - to share passions with others and make their lives shine bright, while recharging ourselves at the same time.

I read this poem in front of the National Speakers Association when I was a new member. The amazing Kelly Swanson (if you have not seen this Goddess speak, go look up her website: https://motivationalspeakerkellyswanson.com immediately, she's a rock star!) was the guest speaker and she was offering a 10 minute spotlight to give advice to people on story telling. It was the first time I'd seen Kelly and nervously I read my poem. She gave me hope and confidence that will stay with me for ever. Her words touched my heart and gave me the courage I needed to keep pursuing my somewhat out of the box dreams. Kelly is not only a phenomenal speaker and story teller, she's a beautiful caring soul, a natural teacher and inspirer. I felt like I met a kindred spirit the night I met Kelly and I may not have stayed the path without her encouragement. She made a difference to me.

Metamorphosis Of A Misfit

You made a difference to me
you're the one I always wanted to be

He smiled, laughed, his emerald eyes a glint
did he know he was my hero, my spark, my flint?

I heard him speak at many events
some were located under big tents

He stood tall, wise, noble and strong
in my eyes, he could do no wrong

His poems rang out, so genuinely sincere
he heard the laughter, what about the tear?

His poetry moved people from present to past
people spoke of him, well after the event's shadow was cast

He made them feel like their life had hope
his laughter filled the room, like an exquisite soap

I followed him wherever he would speak
one time in NZ we climbed Mount Egmont's Peak!

He was in his element, he was born of that land
salt of the earth, that was his brand

His younger days were lived on a dairy farm
he spoke of his life, like it - was a charm

Metamorphosis Of A Misfit

After hearing him speak
a new life - I wanted to seek

I don't know if he knew of my pain
life was grim, I was going insane

Sometimes I would remember something he said
it would pull me back - from joining the dead

Depression, anxiety, no purpose and lost
this is what, clipping my wings, had cost

My birthday was approaching
my birthday was encroaching

Normally this was a favorite celebration
now all I wanted was a recalibration!

In a moment of strength - I reached out in time
I asked him to write me a birthday rhyme

Not long after March 7th - it appeared
the envelope itself seemed revered!

Let me read you the verse
that lifted my curse

That pulled me out of a life of despair
into a life of dreams, in front of you - here!

Metamorphosis Of A Misfit

Let me read you what I had lost sight of in life
let me show you what he saw - instead of strife

To My Sunshine
Sunshine is a name which brings warmth to the face & back
it's so strong it penetrates the heart & soul
with a color so vivid, it creates the image of a well-worn coat & hat
so for someone with this name
they can be proud & bear no shame
A leader, a spiritual healer, someone with vision & wisdom
To make the world & it's people so much kinder
When you obtain financial freedom
you will - like your eagle soar
while catching the thermals & crossing the oceans so vast
please don't fly so far that we can't reach out & knock on your door
I miss you so much - the days are all cloudy
I wish we lived closer - just to say howdy
Your golden smile radiates just like the clown
your happy disposition eliminates the frown
Your beautiful spirituality is happiness exemplified
my wonderful daughter perfect outside and inside
I wish we could spend just a moment or two
as we reminisce about our farm in Kohukohu
My little girl and I, the horse, the cat and dog
wandering through the hills in the early morning fog
it just doesn't get any better than that
money isn't everything - when it comes to joy and happiness
Compared to the human spirit and kindness
money is merely a toy.

Metamorphosis Of A Misfit

Once again, my Dad's voice had inspired my being
he opened my eyes that had become unseeing

My pain was too great, my heart broken forever
until I read his birthday letter

He wanted to make a difference on this earth
go to Africa and feed the starving, not stay in Perth

He wanted to teach English in remote places in China
where they could not afford in life, things finer

He wanted to stop injustice and find a win-win
to provide love in places echoing of sin

His hands were born for helping, his heart for love
his talisman, the Turtle Dove

You made a difference to me, when I was struggling & poor
your words filtered in & filled my core

You made a difference to me, when my life was fragmented
now I live the dream and have a life, centered

Please don't think your words were small
they moulded me to stand tall

May your sincere, humble, introverted soul
always remember your magnificent goal

Metamorphosis Of A Misfit

You made a difference to me
One little starfish, forever set free

Reflection Questions

1. Who has made a difference in your life? This may be a family member, friend, author, speaker or a random stranger that went out of their way, at a time when you most needed what they had to offer.

   _____
   _____
   _____
   _____
   _____
   _____
   _____
   _____

2. What was it that made you feel empowered, supported or inspired by this person?

   _____
   _____
   _____
   _____
   _____
   _____
   _____
   _____

3. Does the person know how they made you feel? What would happen if you told them?

   _____
   _____
   _____
   _____
   _____

4. Who do you make a difference to and how?

5. Who would you love to make more of a difference to and why?

6. What are you capable of when fully supported, encouraged and inspired?

7. When your time on this planet comes to end - how would you want this statement to read: (Your name here) has made a difference in this world by. . .?

-Grand Grief-

You Are A Goddess

This was written when thinking about my best friend Jesmin. We went to High School together, then shared a house, navigating our 17-20's together. Jes, was a medical laboratory assistant at the University Of Western Australia and smart as a whip. She was gorgeous and seemingly had everything going for her in life. Through a series of tragic events, for her, including being made redundant at the University and a break up with her fiancé, Jes left this world. She took some cyanide from work and injected it, to end her life. I speak of this as, almost 20 years after her death, this is still a taboo subject. My dream is to speak of taboo subjects MORE in the desire to create dialogue, understanding, meaning and support. I thought I understood suicide as I'd studied it at length as well as experiencing suicidal thoughts myself, on more than one occasion. My experience with losing my best friend, changed everything I'd studied. I felt like Jes experienced too much emotional pain and wanted it to stop. I think she felt embarrassed, confused and trapped in life. I don't believe she was attempting to hurt anyone or cause them pain. She wanted to stop hers and at the time, that was her only option. I'm not saying what she did was right or wrong. For every person, there are different reasons, feelings, causes for not wanting to live any more. It's as complex and diverse as we are human. Jes was the closest person, I'd ever experienced to having a a sister. When we were out, people often mistook us as sisters, despite our looking very different! She taught me many lessons in life, telling me to NOT do what she did, when it came to relationships! She taught me how to be confident and strong. We experienced much laughter as well as tears in our ten years of knowing each other. Jes died in her early 20's way too young. I was in England when she passed away. We'd had a fight before I left, over a telephone bill. Seems ridiculous now and at the time I remember being devastated, like it was the ending of our friendship. I met Katia in England a week before Jes died. Katia was to become my best friend in the world, interesting how life works out! Jes will always be in my heart and her memory inspires me to make the most out of life.

Metamorphosis Of A Misfit

Look in the mirror and say 3 times, "I am a Goddess!"
we heard this when we were 18 and laughed till we cried no less

Jes and I would taunt each other with this in jest
we were friends forever, the best

I think a lot about our friendship and the good ol' days
that was before she found cyanide and left me in a haze

I can't remember if it was around this time in my despair
that I hungered for self-help material to repair

To patch up the parts of me that felt so broken
and give voice to all my thoughts unspoken

I read of angels and diets, energy and more
I heard about yoga, meditation and how life didn't have to be a chore

It seemed there were techniques and tools to sort me out
I was dying on the inside and wanted to shout

The world seemed unjust and cruel
everything inflamed like fire doused with fuel

I felt salve from the cooling books and their pages
the words like friends that were wise sages

I learned a lot and then became curious like a cat
wanted more information and just like that

Metamorphosis Of A Misfit

It came to me, I should live life to the full!
I knew all too well, that life can be short, what the hell

Might as well go full throttle and have a story worthy life
than struggle, live small, being crippled by strife

I set out to do just that
travelled the world, just me and my pack

I met amazing people and heard many a story
some filled with love, others with glory

I felt alive, invigorated, on top of the world indeed
like a mighty oak grown from just a tiny seed

I felt my self growing, stretching and expanding
this travel could be quite demanding

I felt a freedom I'd never experienced before
the opportunities were like an open door

Beckoning for me to come in
inviting me to share my sin

Dark sides of myself that I kept hidden and deep
were persuaded to come out and take a leap

There were situations I didn't know how I got into
or out of, and yet I flew

Metamorphosis Of A Misfit

Like I had eagle wings and the heart of an ox
to find the jewels, there would be a lot of rocks

With ups and downs, ins and outs, I survived
I made it through and thrived

What would you do if you knew you could not fail
would you run at the chance, or bail?

What would you have to do to live a life that is worthy and sound?
what would it look like and would you have to be lost then found?

I don't know all the answers and one things for sure
there is never just one cure

For everyone's different and that's what makes the world go round
I learned that what I thought was right, was not always sound

There were areas of grey
in every different way

I saw compassion in the flesh
I saw hatred - we didn't mesh

I am a Goddess and you too
we're in this together, so what shall we do?

To make a difference and leave a mark of love on this land
would that not feel grand?

Metamorphosis Of A Misfit

For what else is there apart from happiness, love and healing
I have no interest in a life with a glass ceiling

I want to support, assist and inspire
life's most intimate desire

Peace, love and all that stuff
why can it all get so rough?

I want to protect, heal, comfort and teach
those who are ready willing and able to preach

People who are ready to shout out loud
that enough is enough and stand up proud

I want to be to you, as books have been to me
a savior, an oracle, a whisper and a guide to flee

You are a Goddess, you and me alike
I have no secret powers, just a mike

Take away what you will
and until...

There comes a time when we meet, on this journey of life
may you smell the roses, live to fullest and release all strife

You are a goddess X 3
that message will always stay with me

Reflection Questions

1. When did you last feel powerFULL and amazing?

2. What lights up your spirit and soul?

3. If you knew you could NOT fail, what would you do today?

4. What legacy (mark) do you want to leave in this world?

   _____
   _____
   _____
   _____
   _____
   _____
   _____
   _____

5. When you live BIG, who'll benefit from your message/teachings/creations?

   _____
   _____
   _____
   _____
   _____
   _____
   _____
   _____

6. What's the COST to you, of NOT changing, and living small?

   _____
   _____
   _____
   _____
   _____
   _____
   _____
   _____

7. Who do you know that's successful in an area that you'd like to excel in? What questions could you ask them, to assist you to becoming the success you dream of?

I Remember

This was an exercise I did at a Hay House book writing conference in Chicago. We had 10 minutes to write something, using the title I REMEMBER. After I wrote my 10 minute piece I read it to my friends Susan Young and Sima Dahl and they encouraged me to read it aloud to the whole audience of about 500 people. I did this and it helped to give me confidence that what I wrote was something that moved people. Susan has encouraged me through every stage of this book writing process and without her, it may still be sitting in my computer instead of in your hands!

Metamorphosis Of A Misfit

I remember Kat
how could I forget that

We met in England at a volleyball game
our lives would never be the same

I remember the laughter and the tears
we lived large and shredded our fears

We lived, worked, studied and trained together
overcame any and all weather

I remember her smile - like liquid sun
our journey together, exemplified FUN

I remember her nick name - Swiss Chick
better friend, I could never pick

Time passed by and lives became complicated
Katia developed cancer, our lives devastated

She passed away far too young
her song will always be sung

I remember Katia as a powerful force
she changed my life, redirected my course

My husband Cris, the love of my life
came to me during my grieving and strife

Metamorphosis Of A Misfit

Cris's comfort and words of gold
had me living again, truth be told

Without Kat's passing
I wouldn't have his love everlasting

The death of my friend reconnected us forever
the universe, so very clever

In ways that can be so hard to see at the time
hindsight can be sublime

I know Kat would smile at this turn of events
I think of her always and know she's heaven sent

It broke my heart when she died
many waterfalls, I have cried

Yet I know in her passing she gave me the greatest surprise
that would end my spiral of demise

The surprise of true love
from heaven above

I remember forever my dearest friend
although a new chapter, there was also an end

Metamorphosis Of A Misfit

Reflection Questions

1. Experience this exercise for yourself! Grab a pen and paper or computer and set a timer for 10 minutes. Write whatever comes to mind with the title I Remember. It doesn't need to rhyme, be poetry or even make sense. The idea of the activity is to spark curiosity and maybe there is one word or one 'reminder' that you needed to become aware of? Maybe the gift of this exercise is to allow yourself to write without judgement, something just for you? Whatever your experience, enjoy it and take from it what you will!

   _____
   _____
   _____
   _____
   _____
   _____
   _____
   _____

2. What memories to you recall from childhood?

   _____
   _____
   _____
   _____
   _____
   _____
   _____

3. What was your experience at High School?

   _____
   _____

4. What do you feel when remembering the kiss of someone you love or loved deeply?

5. If you're writing a book, solely based on what you're most passionate about, releasing all thoughts (of right, wrong, should, success, and failure), what will the title be? Why are you passionate about this? What do you hope others may receive from your writing?

6. What's one thing you want to be remembered as?

   _____
   _____
   _____
   _____
   _____
   _____
   _____
   _____
   _____

7. If you were able to speak to the 13 year old you, what would you say? What's one thing you want your younger self to realize?

   _____
   _____
   _____
   _____
   _____
   _____
   _____
   _____
   _____
   _____
   _____
   _____
   _____
   _____
   _____
   _____
   _____

Best Foreign Friend Forever (BFFF)

This poem is very dear to my heart and took some time before I was able to share it as a speaker, without breaking down. The poem speaks for itself and and can be summed up in three words; friendship, adventures, and loss.

Metamorphosis Of A Misfit

The Waifs & Powderfinger
outdoor Ed, the memories linger

I met my friend Katia in England at a volleyball game
I was nannying, she was studying, it was my name

Kirsty was her older sisters name, illegal in the land of the Swiss
this story - I did not want to miss

Turns out, the government regulates naming of a kid
her Mom had to call her Kirsty-Anne for an acceptable bid

We laughed about this and the fact that we were the only two
foreigners in this tiny English town of few

We became instant best friends for ever after
I'm not sure we knew the magnitude of our laughter

We would share over the years
as well as heartache and waterfalls of tears

Kat lived in Switzerland and me in Australia
when we left England we wanted to continue our mania

Our crazy antics of challenge and adventure
we had so much fun in a short time, it was a cure

For our gypsy souls and Goddess spirits of joy
Kat flew to Australia, it worked, my ploy

Metamorphosis Of A Misfit

To entice her there and have her study my course
Leisure Science, my secret source

Of inspiration, adventure and possibilities abound
it was a fail proof system, air tight and sound

For 4 years we worked, lived, studied and played together
we would hardly be apart, ever

People joked about how close we were, a rare find
a bond I can only assume is like siblings of the tightest kind

Then life happened as it does in a way
Kat went back to Switzerland and I, the USA

It was 2001 and Summer Camp Instructor for me
this was the life, I felt so free

My ticket of course went to Switzerland after the US
we couldn't be apart for too long, as you may guess

We planned to somehow be in touch forever
dreaming of duplex houses, a friendship tether

Our future families, the best of friends, it made perfect sense at the time
the memories, taste so sublime

I fell in love in the USA and wanted to go back there to satiate my craving
sooner the better, so I started saving

Metamorphosis Of A Misfit

Then came the day when Kat e-mailed me
She said it was better than talking, see. . .

She had Hodgkinsons, this is cancer
Her spirits were high, she'd find the answer

Positive energies abound
At first, no words to be found

Then came the anger, I was mad at this disease
I wanted to kill it, let me destroy it, PLEASE

Felt so helpless and far away
wanted to do something, more than pray

Time went by, there were ups and downs
sometimes smiles would transform into gnarled frowns. . .

Thinking of Kat
this fu*%$d up turn of events, making her flat

She was 6 foot, blonde, green-eyed beauty and strong
body withered away, it was terminally wrong

This wasn't part of our plan
didn't the universe understand?

Time passed, I was living a life half lived at best
trapped in a dysfunctional relationship, unable to feel blessed

Metamorphosis Of A Misfit

Things were so dire, they were almost fatal for me
I had suicidal thoughts, just wanted to flee

I didn't have the strength or means
I longed for some magic beans

A way to get out of this place, called paradise
I knew deep down I couldn't wear this mask of 'nice'

The day came so horrific - my best friend died
my legs shook uncontrollably, a haunting noise, as I cried

Surrealness overtook me
I had to flee

I couldn't stay here for one more second
life was too short - grief beckoned

It took a little time to dissolve my toxic relationship
moved from that place and saved for a trip

During my grief, no one knew how to console me
I was heading for a breakdown, I wanted people to let me be

Then came an e mail from the love of my life, Cris from Summer Camp
it'd been 9 years since I'd seen him, his words were like a lamp

A light giving me hope and inspiration
I barely recognized this sensation

Metamorphosis Of A Misfit

I'd been living a life insecurely small
I'd forgotten, to stand tall

I was amazed, that his words touched my very soul
to get to the USA, was now my short-term goal

After almost 10 years since seeing this man
I knew he was the one, so flew, then ran. . .

Into his arms, arriving in the USA
I visited, then tears down my face and heart, I left, vowing to return one day

It would be one day soon, as soon as I saved for the fare
I could feel his touch, see his face so clear

In my memories and dreams as well as waking hours
I didn't know how, I knew, I would use all my powers. . .

To get back to Cris and stay with him forever more
it took my best friend's death to re-write my inner lore

To allow me to see, I was living an unauthentic life
filled with trouble, misery and strife

I know Kat would smile at this turn of events
I know without a doubt she was heaven sent

An angel she was with a smile of liquid gold
she touched everyone around her, truth be told

Metamorphosis Of A Misfit

She lived a full life, in too short a time
I'll remember Kat forever - not only in rhyme. . .

Close to my heart, in my spirit for eternity
she changed my life and set me free

Silver linings can be impossible to see in moments of despair
what an incredible gift I was given, my life to repair

The tragedy's not, that my life was crazy
I was unable to see my potential, inability to see through hazy

I wish I could've told Kat more
what she meant to me, I would tell her I adore. . .

Everything about her, that she's an inspiration to me and friends world wide
I imagine she can hear me and I still talk to her with pride

About my accomplishments and when I'm upset
it helps me, get through, a truer friend, I've never met

My best foreign friend forever, Katia Bohn
I still find it impossible, you're gone

Metamorphosis Of A Misfit

Reflection Questions

1. Who's your best friend?
   _____
   _____
   _____
   _____
   _____
   _____
   _____
   _____

2. How did you meet?
   _____
   _____
   _____
   _____
   _____
   _____
   _____
   _____

3. What characteristics does this person have that entitles them to be your bestie?
   _____
   _____
   _____
   _____
   _____
   _____
   _____
   _____

4. What's your favorite outing/experience/adventure with your best friend?

_____
_____
_____
_____
_____
_____
_____
_____

5. How do the two of you resolve conflicts with each other? How does that work out for you?

_____
_____
_____
_____
_____
_____
_____
_____

6. In 5 years time, how do you see your friendship evolving?

_____
_____
_____
_____
_____
_____
_____
_____

7. If you were to write your bestie a letter, telling them why you are grateful they are in your life, what would it say? I **double dare** you to write this letter and post, e mail or deliver it to them. You never know what life has in store and this is an amazing gift to give someone you treasure greatly.

-Mum's The Word-

Marjorie & Sage

I met a beautiful friend in 2001 while traveling in Thailand. I'll call her Sage as she was an old soul in a young spry 26 year old body. She had not long found out she was pregnant and curious about her new journey in life. Tropical paradise barely describes the surroundings of Had Tien, it was like I'd been transported to a magical place where the sea sparkled brighter, delightful food tantalized my tastebuds and people I met, were amazing beings, that shaped and shifted my life. Sage and I would joke about spending the day solving the worlds problems, in reality we spent the morning doing yoga in a sensational tree hut with wooden floors and open walls overlooking the majestic rain forest. We'd then; feast on local fruit, walk, swim, and laugh our way through the day. Some people stayed at The Sanctuary for a day or two, others like myself for a few weeks. Sage was there before I arrived and stayed on after I left. She was on an extensive journey of self discovery and learning. Sage shared with me her childhood and struggles with letting go and releasing her past. She spoke of guilt and her longing for a dream Mom she never had and never would have. Sage knew she was having a girl and wanted to give her daughter a Mom and a life, she'd been denied. She felt torn between cutting ties with her unhealthy Mom and living her life freely. Sage felt guilt around her feelings for family due to the invisible ties that bind blood. We dove into the murky waters of mothers and daughters, the delicate dance that can affect us all. There were many grey areas and no real conclusive decisions made or breakthroughs had. What we shared was an airing out of somewhat of a forbidden topic and feelings. Shining a light into those dark areas that we seldom speak of yet feel relentlessly. It's been 17 years since I've met Sage and still her story stays with me. I send her love and light, that she finds peace around her feelings and love within her beautiful heart and that of her daughters'.

Metamorphosis Of A Misfit

Sage blamed her mum for her screwed up life
Marjorie, the cause of her strife

There were times she hated her and her fashion
more times that she hated herself with a passion

Sage saw black, Marjorie saw white
she felt riddled with spite

Her body would quiver, she'd run
this is how she won

It was the only way she knew how to control her emotion
she'd run till she pulled muscles, it worked like a potion

Sage would d return, sore, exhausted yet calm
like a festering wound smothered with balm

She was unable to see Marjorie's pain, her point of view
too much hatred, rage and so green and new

Their relationship, not clear, there was victory and defeat
pain mixed with sweet

Heartache, suicide threats and emotional abuse
this went both ways, a slippery slide with the threat of a noose

Metaphorical noose, a threat all the same
Sage knew she was the one to blame

Metamorphosis Of A Misfit

Marjorie didn't want a baby, her husband did
Sage felt like a screwed up, damaged kid

Sage's emotions were volatile and would attack without warning
one minute happy, the next storming

It wasn't all bad, that would've made it easier for sure
there were times of fun, it was no cure

Sage felt like she caused Marjorie's life to be, half lived and deprived
one that without her, she would've thrived

Sage felt like Marjorie gave up her dreams to be a parent
she felt this deeply, the feeling - resent

Marjorie had her issues and Sage her line
they clashed and crashed never knowing if things would ever be fine

Sage understands more now and forgives Marjorie for her imperfections
she forgives herself for her cutting inflictions

Sage caused Marjorie pain and Marjorie her, just the same
sometimes Sage still wanted to blame

Then remind herself, she makes a choice, for how she's to live
time to stop the blame game and forgive

Sage works on this each and every day
will she ever feel freedom fully? There must be a way

Metamorphosis Of A Misfit

How can 40 years of life still be stuck in the past
Sage wishes she could erase it, have a clean slate that'd last

Although then she would not be, herself
and surely thats not being free, or good for your health

Marjorie taught Sage some of the greatest lessons of her life
some, cutting like a knife. . .

Others so gentle, compassionate and kind
Sage will remember, keeping them foremost in her mind

There you have it, two beings bonded by family ties
time to release the hurt - say goodbyes

Maybe these two need rules & regulations
guides and realizations

Maybe their life will change with Sage's new baby
maybe - maybe

Sage's heart was protected
her love for Marjorie rejected

Sage always had hope, she'd forget the past
the sparkle of newness would shine and last

Until Marjorie would again shatter her spirit
Sage, adjusting would set a new limit

Metamorphosis Of A Misfit

Time will tell how their stories end
when I know their fate, I note I'll send

I pray they find peace in their souls
reach all their life goals

May they find a way
to redesign their relationship, not stray

May they find pleasure and fun
feel the brightness from the sun

I dream a life of love for these two
life that despite the years, is brand new

Reflection Questions

1. What does your relationship with your parent/s look like?

   _____
   _____
   _____
   _____
   _____
   _____
   _____
   _____

2. What relationship do you have with your kids or kids you interact with in life?

   _____
   _____
   _____
   _____
   _____
   _____
   _____
   _____

3. What would you say to your parent/s if if was SAFE and possible to do so? What is it, you really need them to hear?

   _____
   _____
   _____
   _____
   _____
   _____

4. If you were able to tell your 13 year old self one thing, what would it be?

　

5. Who do you know that has a similar experience in childhood to you? In what ways, has it shaped your lives?

　

6. What blessings do you have from your childhood?

7. If you were to write yourself a healing letter, from your parent/s what would it say?

Momma Bear

This poem was written when Carolyn Flyer (intuitive coach) asked me these questions; "What do you do for self care? What is it that you need?" These questions sent me into a spin, as I didn't know how to answer them. I thought about what I did for self care and it made me more stressed, like I had to add more onto my full plate. I couldn't even figure out what I wanted or needed. I knew something wasn't right, I didn't know how to get out of the stuck place I was in. I didn't know how to reach out for help. I reflected on how I felt within the different parts within myself. I took some time to imagine what it would feel like to be relaxed, rejuvenated and recalibrated. From this place I worked backward figuring out small steps to take, to get me to that beautiful place. As Mommas of humans and pets, we can go through a variety of stages and stuck-ness, sweet successes and super challenging dark places. This poem's diving into my inner most thoughts and reflections on being a Momma and figuring out my new place and direction in life.

Metamorphosis Of A Misfit

Momma Bear Momma Bear
what do you fear?

Is it that you'll not be enough?
how much stuff

Will it take to feel worthy
to embrace your curvy

Momma Bear shape
do you have a magical cape

One you put on and feel secure
a cape that is like a magical lure

It allows you to be SUPER MOM
to face the world and then some

Momma Bear Momma Bear
how do you self-care?

Is this even a thing that you do?
what does it mean for you?

Momma Bear, Momma Bear where do you go
when your deep in the depths of life's flow

Are you grounded and strong?
or like a game of ping pong?

Metamorphosis Of A Misfit

Bouncing back and forth over the net
never feeling like your needs are met

Momma Bear, Momma Bear, how are YOU?
ever feel trapped, in feeling BLUE?

Do you wear a mask?
hide from the task?

Life can be hectic and crazy
ever feel a little lost and hazy?

Momma Bear, Momma Bear
do you feel me near?

I'm your inner most thoughts and fears
your outer most support crew and peers

Momma Bear, Momma Bear, did you sign up for this
the crazy, messy, eternal bliss?

Do you feel conflicted in your every move
like a deer in headlights, out of your groove?

Do you feel derailed and a little lost
wondering how you'll cover the cost?

Parenthood is a multifaceted gem stone
sometimes sparkly, other-times monotone

Metamorphosis Of A Misfit

There's no playbook of magical convention
sometimes those babies, need your attention

Despite the time, convenience or place
you're in the parenthood race

This race is for life and love magnanimous
where your win, is a heartfelt kiss

There are no rules or regulations
it's full of explosive sensations

Some grand, others, not so much
do you always feel, in a rush?

Where did your previous life go?
what happened to ebb and flow?

Momma Bear, Momma Bear, what do you need?
what delightful, whimsical seed

Can be planted within your soul
what is your end goal?

Momma Bear, Momma Bear, how do you ask?
how do you wear your vulnerability mask?

How do you access much needed self care
when life seems like an emergency flare?

Metamorphosis Of A Misfit

Do you have loving support around you
or is your life more like a zoo?

Screeching, smelly and staring
judgement rather than caring

Momma Bear, Momma Bear, do you feel isolation
how are you dealing with that deep frustration?

Ever feel confusion and guilt
like a heavy weighted quilt

Draping over you, it's hard to move forward
like a strict menacing land lord

Momma Bear, Momma Bear, are your needs met?
what do you want to catch in your net?

Is it butterflies and peace
or a mixture of sweet release?

Ever wish you could just escape for a bit
fly away with a magical kit

Return, rejuvenated, revived and renovated
exhilarated and motivated

Momma Bear, Momma Bear, why do I care?
because I am you, we're one dear

Metamorphosis Of A Misfit

We're united in our life
sisters in our strife

Daughters, all of us unite
join in our mighty might

Support each other where we can
collaboratively make a plan

To live a life, well worth living
to be ever present and giving

To honor our struggles and success
to embrace the delightful mess

That is being a Momma Bear
we are all there

Together in our dark places
figuring out the rules at furious paces

Momma Bear, Momma Bear, are we there
how will we know and is it near?

We are all unique
in what we seek

I wish for you dreams and love and rest
to not take the test

Metamorphosis Of A Misfit

Of life so seriously regulated and dull
break out of your outermost hull

Shed and shine bright
see with new eyes a different sight

For how we see will change our view
we know this to be true

Is it a cloudy day
or is it universe's way

Telling us to take a break
for goodness sake!

Not everything is as it seems
sometimes life is like dreams. . .

A little hazy or crystal clear
far off and distant or near

Momma Bear, Momma Bear, breathe in and out
dance around and shout, shout, SHOUT

For the world to hear your Momma Bear Cry
to make it obvious, your WHY

So everyone knows why you work so relentlessly
your WHY is your vision you see

Metamorphosis Of A Misfit

My WHY is to take people from stuck to sublime
to make their valuable time

On this planet matter
to feel more focus, less shatter

To live a story worthy life
feeling more abundance, less strife

Momma Bear, Momma Bear, feel your sisterhood
a supportive tribe of angels doing good

They'll lift you up, to where you belong
together you'll sing the most magnificent song

From your heart, soul and mind
your purpose you will find

Relax Momma Bear
release your fear

TRUST
ADJUST

A new day is dawning
it's a fresh start every morning

Choose how your story will read
select what type of seed

Metamorphosis Of A Misfit

You'll plant in your characters soul
you get to write your goal

Join hands with me
set your spirit free

Give yourself permission
to make another decision

When things don't turn out right
you can choose to lose sight

Or light a flame
burn the shame

Forge a new direction in your brick road
re-write your code

Program your life, so it works for you
be amazed at what you can do

Momma Bear, Momma Bear, take a deep breath
there's only one certainty in life and that's death

Know that anything can be changed
re-scripted, rearranged

Parenting is too important for a stifled voice
think of it more as multiple choice

Metamorphosis Of A Misfit

Although there is no clear right or wrong
as you will have, your own sweet song

Live this day as if it were a puzzle piece key
what is it you're dying to see?

Momma Bear, Momma Bear, you are enough
despite what you think, you're super tough

You have enough to make a difference
to shape a life and be of significance

Take care of yourself on this journey of gold
your tiny beings are shaped in your mold

Reflection Questions

1. What area of your life to you feel immense responsibility? This may be as a parent, a care giver, a guardian, a pet owner, a job you have or a variety of other things!

   _____
   _____
   _____
   _____
   _____
   _____
   _____

2. For some of us, great responsibility goes hand in hand with stress. What do you do to manage stress? How's that working out for you?

   _____
   _____
   _____
   _____
   _____
   _____
   _____

3. How do you integrate different parts of yourself? If you feel conflicted, how do you align your feelings? How do you make a decision when faced with opposing solutions?

   _____
   _____
   _____
   _____

_____

_____

_____

4. Is there anyone in your family or friend circle that believes self care is selfish? What are your thoughts surrounding self care?

_____

_____

_____

_____

_____

_____

_____

_____

5. When you get depleted, you can't be your best for yourself or others. Who is most affected, by you being depleted and running on empty?

_____

_____

_____

_____

_____

_____

_____

6. When you feel; energized, invigorated, excited and motivated, what are you capable of?

_____

_____

_____

7. When was the last time you felt this way? What was the result? What are steps you can take to get to this motivated state?

I'm Not Okay

I wrote this poem when our baby girl was 6 months. I was struggling with the adjustment of being a Momma, dealing with cancer and not progressing as fast as I wanted to as an entrepreneur. I struggled with being a wife and uncertain who I was most days. I felt like a warmed up zombie and I don't like zombies! I wanted to be everything and do everything and live some magical fantasy that I constructed in my head. This was way too much of a task for me. I didn't have a lot of family support or childcare as my family lived in Australia and asking for help is not one of my talents! I didn't mention that I had also published and crowd funded a book when our baby was five months old, I was burnt out and in desperate need of a break. I told myself that because I was breast feeding, that it would be impossible for me to get away for even a day and that my friends would not want to be bothered by me asking them to baby sit. I will add that as I got better at asking friends for assistance, they were always so gracious and amazing and if they were available, they'd always say yes. My friend Mary Helen Conroy and her partner Mary D, Francis Parker and Theresa Kim were angels when I needed them the most.

Our daughter Zennia is now 19 months and I recently had another break down! My friends Mary Helen Conroy and Jacy Imilkowski, booked an all day spa trip for the three of us, gifting this to me as I was stressed about not having any speaking gigs. They touched my heart and helped heal an old wound I have around believing I don't have any 'true friends' (whatever that means!) and reminded me to keep reaching out and sharing, despite my instinct to go hide under that rock until every thing is perfectly perfect! They did what only 'true friends' can do; they loved me, for being me, made sure I had sound supports in place, gave me sage advice, let me vent, boosted my precious ego, and made me laugh.

Metamorphosis Of A Misfit

I put on my smile and say I'm fine
I wish I could drink some wine

To drown my sorrows and make sense of the stress
to wish my life was not a mess

It is and I can't stand it
I can't cope and my stomach's a pit

My perfectionistic standards fall around me
I feel like a fraud and want to flee

Having a 6-month-old daughter and a business too
I thought I could juggle and try a different shoe

I thought I could do it all and make it work
I thought I was invincible, turns out I'm a jerk!

It occurred to me suddenly one day
crying at nothing you might say

Yet the tears were important and vivid
my spirit livid

Friends and family would ask me "how are you?"
I would autonomously reply "good, how are you?"

Inside I knew it was a lie
there was a part of me that wanted to die

Metamorphosis Of A Misfit

Just temporarily, to have some rest
stop my mind and this awful test

The test I set for myself every day
judging myself in a perfectionistic way

I'm not enough and never will be
I feel trapped and I lost the key

I can't figure out how to make my business financial
I feel like a terrible parent, so unsubstantial

My relationship is suffering, I'm so tired
I hate myself and feel wired

Opposing feelings of exhaustion and high
I wish I could figure out why

I wish I could control my life and emotions
I want to squelch the commotions

I cry at the smallest thing
I want to sing

I want to be the best role model for my baby
I want to show her I'm a success and maybe

She will believe that she's capable of anything
she'll feel in her core that she can sing

Metamorphosis Of A Misfit

That her voice will be heard
her ideas and dreams are not absurd

I want her to be proud
for her spirit to be loud

I feel like an intruder in my own skin
It's like I have an invisible twin

One of us is fairly normal and calm
the other is crazy and belongs on the Funny Farm

Part of me is sane and stable
the other is like a three-legged table

That at any time could fall down
turning my smile into a dark frown

So when I tell you, I'm OK in my shell
I want to be and I'm not, can you tell?

I hide it so well that sometimes I fool my being
I'm a pretender and not all seeing

I put on a mask
to deal with the task

The task of living up to my expectations
of setting goals that exceed rationalizations

Metamorphosis Of A Misfit

I get mad sometimes at not having time
I get frustrated with not being sublime

I get jealous when I see my friends progress
I feel my life regress

I wish I were somewhere I'm not
I wish I was further along on my dream slot

What does this mean
I want to be seen

Yet I want to hide and have my imperfections hidden
I want to pretend they are forbidden

Maybe if I stay small and quiet
no one will find out my truth, I can hide it

Maybe I can forget my dream
stay unseen

I don't have the answer
I'm tired of cancer

Not just the melanoma on my jaw
the cancer of my imagination that's like a festering sore

My mind can be so damaging and cruel
some days are like an uphill gruel

Metamorphosis Of A Misfit

So when you ask me if I'm OK
I'll do my best to be honest today

I'll do my utmost to be truthful and clear
to feel my feelings near

To face my gremlins and re-write my story
to trust and adjust and embrace the glory

As well as the dark bits and rough edges
I'll do my best to stay away from ledges

To stop from running, hiding and fleeing
to face my fears and become all seeing

To work on the Mom I aspire to be
to release negativity and set my spirits free

Am I OK? Somedays are better than others
will I be OK? Just like all mothers. . .

Sometimes I'm overjoyed with love and pride
other days I want to get on another ride

I'm OK with not being okay all the time
I can live with not being eternally sublime

What I need is time and space
to escape my stuck place

Metamorphosis Of A Misfit

I need support in living my dreams
I need to keep showing up on teams

Of wonderful networking crew
to be in the presence of people like you

To hold me accountable and support me in living large
my own supportive entourage

Thank you for listening and allowing my voice
thank you for reminding me I have a choice

Are you - OK?
May you have a story sensational day

Metamorphosis Of A Misfit

Reflection Questions

1. When was the last time you felt like you were not ok? What was going on around you to have this feeling?

   _____
   _____
   _____
   _____
   _____
   _____
   _____
   _____

2. What lets you know - that you are not ok?

   _____
   _____
   _____
   _____
   _____
   _____
   _____
   _____

3. What support system, tools, techniques do you have in place when you are not ok?

   _____
   _____
   _____
   _____
   _____
   _____
   _____
   _____

4. Do you notice any patterns when you experience not being ok?

   _____
   _____
   _____
   _____
   _____
   _____
   _____
   _____

5. What do you need from friends and family when you are struggling emotionally? What can they do or say (not say) to best support you?

   _____
   _____
   _____
   _____
   _____
   _____
   _____
   _____

6. If money were no issue, what would you do to make yourself feel better, relaxed and rejuvenated? How can you find a work around, to make any of these things happen in your current circumstance?

   _____
   _____
   _____
   _____
   _____

7. What is the cost to you of not 'putting on your oxygen mask first?' The cost of serving others needs before your own and running on empty?

-Kinesthetic-

Run To Me

How is it possible to forget about what you love doing? I know I'm not alone in this, as I've had coaching clients that have done the same thing. It may sound crazy and that doesn't make it not true! My earliest memories are of running. I was involved in some sort of little kid running club and when I was 6, we moved to a dairy farm where I remember running up the hills and down the tracks. When moving to Australia with my family, I'd run the streets and the sand. Running was my mental health partner and not only kept me strong and fit, it soothed my crazy mind. It assisted me with what I now label; anger, anxiety, depression, and frustration. It gave me an outlet to deal with life. I was very competitive with myself and whatever training plan I'd created or following, I would stick to it no matter what. Problem was, that I grew up with the belief of 'no pain - no gain,' this resulted in a lot of serious injuries. In my late 20's I stopped running regularly and life went on. Tofe Evans wrote a book that reminded me to rekindle my love of running and the rest is history!

Metamorphosis Of A Misfit

"Run to me" I heard her call
I replied, "no I'll fall"

All I could think of was pain
and more and more I was going insane

Running used to be my salve
my pressure valve

To stop from exploding and keep me in check
to give me reason not to wreck

My life and stay on track
now I look back

I wonder why I stopped, how it happened to be
it was slowly and gradually

That I stopped wearing running shoes
feeling like I'd only lose

Telling myself I was protecting my knees
give me a break, please

This was an excuse and no real reason
to use the season

Of winter as a reason not to run
it used to be so much fun

Metamorphosis Of A Misfit

Some of my best memories are from running hard
for 15 years, I was barred

From running in my life
fear was rife

The main reason for me stopping my sport
my body used to be taught

Yet with that came injury
now softness, weakness and insecurity

My limited belief was that running caused injury and pain
now I realize it makes me sane

Reading Tofe Evans book
allowed me a second look

At my reason for being stagnant and slow
never wanting to go

The extra mile to feel fine
release my stressors, feel sublime that's mine

I used to look at runners and scoff at their ridiculous gear
I mean really, shorts in snow, I fear

I would die of cold
I'm not sold

Metamorphosis Of A Misfit

On running in the winter months outdoors
doesn't mean there aren't other floors

That can't be run upon, even indoor
like a gym or stairs or more

Options are endless when I'm open to see
now, I run with glee

I'm unfit and slow
doesn't mean I can't go

Join in the fun, train to my best ability
and slowly build up the agility

I signed up for a half marathon in June
that's 14 weeks soon!

I know I can do it, not fast
yet finishing with a blast

For an accomplishment, proving to myself that I'm strong
that my limited beliefs were wrong

"Come run with me" the voice said
I was led

To follow this road
design my code

Metamorphosis Of A Misfit

Of how to make running work for me
I feel set free

Released from excuses and feeling sad
telling myself it was just a fad

I had when I was younger, fitter and better
that's simply not true, I'll write a letter. . .

Reminding my mind that age and fitness is no reason
to commit treason

Betraying myself for what I know is a desire
to run, be free and fly higher

"Run to me" I heard her say
so I did and come what may!

Reflection Questions

1. What's an activity, hobby or sport that you used to love?

   _____
   _____
   _____
   _____
   _____
   _____
   _____
   _____

2. How did it make you feel? Why were you drawn to it and do you still do it?

   _____
   _____
   _____
   _____
   _____
   _____
   _____
   _____

3. Who in your life do you admire for the activities they do and what stops you from doing the same thing?

   _____
   _____
   _____
   _____
   _____
   _____
   _____
   _____

4. How will it feel in 6 months time when you've been consistently doing the movement activity of your choice? Let's face it, 6 months is going to pass regardless of what you do or don't do, so you might as well utilize it!

_____
_____
_____
_____
_____
_____
_____
_____

5. How will you feel differently after 6 months of your desired activity? What will let you know, you've changed or shifted?

_____
_____
_____
_____
_____
_____
_____
_____

6. What support, accountability, apps or clubs are there out there, for what it is that you love?

_____
_____
_____
_____

7. Who will you most inspire by creating and sculpting a more awesome you? Why is this important for you? What is the cost of staying exactly the same?

Finding Your Authentic Self

I'm amazed at how starting my business, opened a flood gate of self discovery! The majority of these poems were inspired by my entrepreneurial journey and this one is no exception. I remember getting to a point in my business where I wondered who I really was and was I going in the right direction. I wanted to really explore who I was and who I wanted to be. I wanted to make sure that the present me and the future me were in some sort of alignment. I wanted to be conscious of the clothes I wore, the style I adopted, the way I presented myself to the world, my family and myself. I was curious that I did not know exactly who I was and wanted to change that. I wanted a life that I had designed with love, compassion and joy. I wanted my business to reflect the sort of business that I admired. I was tired of feeling lost and disconnected. I now see that my authentic self changes with time and life circumstances yet the essence is always the same. It's this essence that I was attempting to capture, bottle and label. I wanted something tangible that I could use as a guide to assist me in making decisions and choosing direction.

Metamorphosis Of A Misfit

Sounds easy doesn't it?
don't you just listen and sit?

Tune in to some inner wisdom
and all is revealed in a magical system

I mean how difficult can it be
to find out about me?

I've been alive for 43 years
I have worries and I have cares

I have needs, desires like everyone else around
what makes me lost and them found?

How do I even begin to figure out who I am
where do I start and can I just swallow a web cam

That would solve it all
it could take some video footage and I would stand tall

Knowing I had proof, of what goes on, inside of me
that would surely set me free

So the webcam idea was not that tasty
maybe I was a little hasty

Let me re-evaluate how to find me
seriously

Metamorphosis Of A Misfit

Well let's start right there
I'm not that serious, I do care

I have an element of serious, yet it's not defining
I think I'm more fun and less fine dining

I'm more artsy and environmental
I do love an Indian dahl made with lentil

Maybe I'm less pencil and more, skirts that flow
how do I really know?

What if I'm guessing, yeah that's what I said
what if I'm making it all up in my head?

What lets me know an authentic thought from an ego one
what allows me to feel amazingly shiny like the sun?

There it is, that feeling word
sound absurd?

That's the key
for me

Simple it may sound
it feels homeward bound

Like coming back to a place that is truly me
I place I can feel, myself and be set free

Metamorphosis Of A Misfit

Not the small me that is scared of her own shadow
the confident bold me that skips through a meadow

The me that soaks up the sun
and see's life as fun

The me, that looks in the mirror and sees beauty
then with a wry smile says "hey cutie"

And laughs and laughs at life's little amusements
my hair being in lighter tints

I've been all sorts of colors, some were a reach
authentic to me seems to come in a bottle and bleach!

Is it ok, that authentic is not natural and what I was born with?
I want this to be true and not based in myth

I want to believe that whatever makes me feel beautiful
and joyous is what my authentic self is, despite not being natural

So, I'm getting closer
I'm being nosier

Digging into my own business, to see what makes me tick
what really lights me up, what is, my best pick

I start with easy things like clothing fun
this used to make me want to run

Metamorphosis Of A Misfit

Hide because I felt ugly and too big
like I'd lost myself, morphed into a pig!

Now I get excited and only purchase clothing, I feel amazing in
if I get home and don't love them, they get the recycling bin!

My authentic self knows, what makes her shine
she knows what makes her feel divine

My inner self knows, the work I do is pure love, not a flit
or a flighty fancy, it's totally worth it

Every struggle and set back
I know it's of vital importance to get back on track

To live my life as a shining example
of an exquisite sample

Of what my life can be
when I set my focus to my authentic me!

I'm recognizing that future woman, some
the one I'm working on, to become

The woman that makes me feel proud
the one that shines and sings out loud

That's my true authentic self in a nut shell
she's the one, that I can tell. . .

Metamorphosis Of A Misfit

Will be successful in all aspects of her life
she can differentiate between calm and strife

She wakes with a smile and sleeps sound
she overcomes with ease every little mound

She floats gracefully through her day
that's me, what can I say

It feels great to be on a path heading toward home
to know I'm not facing things alone

To have that support, guidance and light
to be prepared to take flight

Live my life to the best of my ability
watch me move through the agility

Course that life provides
now I'm equipped with my guides

I check in when I feel lost
and ask them, what is the cost?

Of not being truly me
tell me of what you see

I use that information
to get on and off at the perfect station

Metamorphosis Of A Misfit

I'm now guided and can see the light

at the end of the tunnel, its beautifully bright

what will you do when you discover her

what will change, what makes you purr?

Set yourself free to find who you are

you will shine bright like the most phenomenal star

Reflection Questions

1. Who are you? If you were describing yourself as a character in a story, what traits would you have?

   _____
   _____
   _____
   _____
   _____
   _____
   _____
   _____
   _____

2. How do you know when you are being authentic? What lets you know?

   _____
   _____
   _____
   _____
   _____
   _____
   _____
   _____
   _____

3. When you see someone who is not being authentic, what let's you know?

   _____
   _____
   _____
   _____
   _____
   _____

4. Why is it important for you to be your authentic self?

_____
_____
_____
_____
_____
_____
_____
_____

5. When were you in a situation where you were not your authentic self? How did this feel?

_____
_____
_____
_____
_____
_____
_____
_____

6. When you see someone shining with authenticity, how does that make you feel? What gift are they giving you by being their authentic self?

_____
_____
_____
_____
_____

7. If you were to know your authentic super powers, what would they be?

Power Of Play

I love including play in my presentations. I also used it when I was a teacher. it's so much fun using play as a tool for learning. There is incredible research on the importance of play for adults and I believe it's an untaped resource for solving many issues we have in our personal and work lives. When I remember to play and incorporate it into my schedule, the quality of my day skyrockets! It's my dream to spread the play message as far and wide as possible and create a ripple effect of play throughout the world!

Metamorphosis Of A Misfit

What would make your day?
would you love to have more play?

What if you lived like a little kid?
embracing life and not caring what you did

Dancing around like a maniac
loving every minute, getting your childhood back

Embracing, fun freedom and creativity
seeing eyes through naivety

What if you stopped your stress in it's tracks?
jumped up and down and ate some fun snacks?

Imagine swinging so high on swings
feeling like a bird with soaring wings

What will it feel like to play free?
want to try it with me?

We can do it now, just for one second
close your eyes and feel it beckon

That feeling of play igniting your heart
it's time to make a fresh start

Let go of your troubles, release them into the air
throw your hands up, like you just don't care!

Metamorphosis Of A Misfit

Play can recalibrate your soul
make a mountain into a mole

Turning the huge into something insignificant
turning life into the magnificent

You can tell me excuses all day long
you can tell me your troubles and why they are wrong

I'll tell you there is always someone worse off than you
you get to choose to start anew

How's your life working out for you?
if its not freakin fantastic then it's time to renew

Gain insight, cut loose, live it up to the full
make your own rule

For how you will truly live
what do you have you can give

Life's not over till it's over for you and your crew
I hear you have your troubles, I have mine too

From cancer to my best friend killing herself at 23
don't feel sorry for me

My worries don't end there
and I know without a doubt that my life is fair

Metamorphosis Of A Misfit

Compared to others I'm blessed from above
living a life peaceful as a turtle dove

So when I cry a tear
because fear is near

I have a choice to choose a piece of play
to make me smile even though things don't go my way

I found out I had cancer when I was 5 months pregnant
melanoma being one of the few cancers that can pass from Momma to infant

My best friend like a sister to me, died from cancer in her thirties
our Sky Dog was hit by a car and spent 13 days in ICU with multitude hurties!

He's now full of titanium and we have a $20,000 canine
he's a lucky pup and walked the line

We are so lucky he's still with us and every time I drive our car that's falling apart
I smile and know that having Sky in our lives is way more than a transportation cart

There is always room for a little play
maybe it will just make your day

No matter what goes on in your life
you can choose play or choose strife

It doesn't mean your being selfish or escaping forever
it's a tool for learning, relieving, releasing and a lever

Metamorphosis Of A Misfit

To get you going in a different direction than despair
no one wants to stay stuck there

Always have a dream to bounce toward
know some tools to propel you forward

Do you even know, what play is for you?
it's easy to forget, I do!

Maybe it's blowing bubbles or dancing all crazy
maybe it's getting a fog machine and seeing all hazy

Maybe it's writing notes and leaving them in trees
for people to find and maybe the breeze

Will carry them to who needs them the most
maybe your writing will stick to a post

Play may be dressing up in the most fabulous of attire
walking the street and feeling desire

Play for you may be art creations
mixing media sensations

Play may be adventures of the adrenalin kind
or playing music that sounds perfect in your mind

Play is whatever you want it to be
it's doing for no reason to set your mind free

Metamorphosis Of A Misfit

Play often, regularly and with friends
play to make amends

Play till your heart sings
play to soothe the stings

Play to teach others in your life
how to disintegrate strife

Play to show there's another way
to release a pressure valve in your day

Play play and play some more
play till you feel it in your core

Play to activate your super powers
play to take time and smell the flowers

Play to make someone else's day
play to shout HOORAY!

Play play play
it's the only way

To bring joy, fun exuberance, back into your path
to remind you to remember to laugh

Play to learn what makes you feel best
play will take care of the rest

Metamorphosis Of A Misfit

Reflection Questions

1. What gets you all tied up in knots, stressed, sad and stuck?

   _____
   _____
   _____
   _____
   _____
   _____
   _____
   _____

2. What have you done in your past that bought relief, laughter and love in your heart?

   _____
   _____
   _____
   _____
   _____
   _____
   _____
   _____

3. Who will love to play with you, to go on adventures and laugh till your sides hurt?

   _____
   _____
   _____
   _____
   _____
   _____
   _____
   _____

4. What is the most playful thing you have done in the last 30 days?

_____
_____
_____
_____
_____
_____
_____
_____

5. What did you love to do when you were younger? What was your favorite way to play?

_____
_____
_____
_____
_____
_____
_____
_____

6. What will happen if you budget in 5 minutes a day of play? That's 35 minutes a week of playtime!

_____
_____
_____
_____
_____
_____
_____
_____

7. What's the cost to you, of NOT creating play time in your life?

-Truths-

Trust The Universe

This poem came from two intertwined events. One was still feeling the sting of not being paid for work completed for an insurance company I worked with. The second came from, money stress! I was building my business and getting so bogged down, burned out and stressed. I was tempted and terrified of getting a 'real job!' I knew from experience that this was not a divine path for me and yet the secure paycheck from working somewhere, ANYWHERE was really appealing and tantalizing. I was struggling desperately with who I was, what my mission on earth was and where the universe was taking me. I felt less than and like a failure as I was not bringing in the finances (or any finances) that I had dreamed of. My fear of FAILING was huge and there was that pivotal moment of deciding what to do next. Would I listen to the Gremlins in my head and my stressed out body and mind or would I dig deep, trust and take a leap. This feeling has come up over and over, in different shapes and forms in my entrepreneurial journey. I'm blessed to now have the support and techniques to manage it, when it rears it's unicorn head!

Metamorphosis Of A Misfit

Trust the universe, what crap!
does the universe know, I have no map?

I'm lost - confused
feeling abused

By life, people I thought were friends
I don't know how to make amends

How do I fix this mess?
just trust the universe I guess!

How do I stop my body shaking with rage
I feel it eating at me, can't focus, or engage

My thoughts bombarded with events so biting
put me in a ring and I'll start fighting

That's how mad, hurt and cheated I feel
I know I'm right, this sh*% is real!

It makes my blood boil feeling injustice done
makes me want to escape and run

Away from the situation, from life
to avoid pain and strife

That worked in my younger days
now in my 40's, it doesn't work, the same ways!

Metamorphosis Of A Misfit

So trust the universe I hear you say
I want to mock, snicker, snare and may

Yet I know from experience that this statement is true
the hurt I'm experiencing that's what's making me blue

I know I can trust the universe and all will be sublime
I know this situation was really just a matter of time

There are bigger and better things in store for me, t's just a ploy
things in the future will take me closer to my authenticity and joy

So although I feel pain now and conflict and hard done by
when I trust and release my worry to the universe, I will sigh

Sigh with relief and freedom and excitement for new opportunity
deep down, I know this is all in divine order, to set me free

So thanks universe for your tests and trials
thanks for allowing me, to go the extra miles

I'd not be the person I am today without my life situation
I wouldn't be able to share my experiences and inspire others or even a nation!

Ego speaks loud in my head
it wants the injustice dead

It shouts, hurts and screams to be heard
I know this is not my true self, that's absurd

Metamorphosis Of A Misfit

Yes it's part of me, yet it doesn't define me as a being
the universe is love and all seeing

There's my business and universe business, a line in the sand
not to be crossed, this my sanity will demand

Thank you universe for being you
without your guidance, I may never have taken flight and flew

When you trust the universe, what does that free you from?
stress, mess, control, an unexploded emotional bomb?

Traveling by myself in my twenties for three years
it helped me have trust, let go of my fears

Many a foreign land
and adventures on hand

Some joyful, some terrifying
without trust I wouldn't have experienced living, only dying. . .

Dying a small death inside, knowing I'd lived only half a life
there would've been way less fun and double the strife!

So thank you universe for your blessings and more
I'm grateful and thankful for, that 'other' door

The door that opens to the sublime
energy mass of love, safety & belonging, just at the right time!

Reflection Questions

1. When was the last time you trusted the universe, when something was out of your control?

   _____
   _____
   _____
   _____
   _____
   _____
   _____
   _____

2. How do you feel when you have no control of a situation and need FAITH, PRAYER, and or TRUST?

   _____
   _____
   _____
   _____
   _____
   _____
   _____
   _____

3. Think of a time in your life when 'life happened,' what was the outcome? Over time, did your feelings change about this situation?

   _____
   _____
   _____
   _____
   _____

4. What if you strongly believed, the universe 'had your back,' that your FAITH, whatever that means for you, was there for you 110% and that no decision you made was wrong?

5. When you trust others in your life, what ends up happening? What if you trusted MORE?

6. Who do you trust most in your life? How much do you trust yourself?

7. What are you capable of with 110% trust that you are on the right path? If I wave a magic wand and you felt completely confident and secure in your decisions, how will that affect your life?

Trials To Transformations

This poem was written after I completed work for a large health insurance company and was not paid. The way they dealt with the situation was unprofessional to say the least and my tender heart was broken. I'd worked for the company for a year and built friendships there. I was shocked and shattered when I discovered they were not paying me for work I'd already done. I learned several lessons during this time, one being to get a contract signed and follow up when invoices have not been paid. The best outcome was, the kick in the pants I needed to go out on my own and start my business. I was using this company as a security blanket, as it was well known in the area. My friend Kim Kotecki and I were filming her Recalibration Reals interview and one of the things she bought up was this saying "what is NOW possible?" This statement is perfect for this occurrence! What is possible NOW? I realized, this wasn't a company I was proud to work for, it didn't fit my values and morals. NOW I had an opportunity to create a work environment I loved! Had this MESS not happened, I may still be there today! Too afraid to let go of the security and set myself free. "Mr Hindsight is a wonderful thing" my Dad would often tell me! Indeed hindsight is amazing and NOW I feel blessed for the MESS and grateful that it aided me in taking a stand, a risk, and a chance. It allowed me to fly and be free!

Metamorphosis Of A Misfit

Right now I feel more trial than transform

I know it won't last and I'll be back to perform

It's easy for me to lose sight of this in the thick of trial and tribulation

I just want to ride away and jump off at some random station

I want to flee

to feel free

I want to shrink and minimize, I'm ready for flight

I want to be prepared no matter what my plight

Feeling sore, hurt and down

my smile fading, transforming into a frown

Weather seems to match my mood

dreary, drizzly and really quite rude!

So I sit here with a hot water bottle to sooth my aches

I reflect of the future and past mistakes

I know mentally that this trial will transform and that there is a silver lining

somehow at this stage, it's not comforting so I sit here pining

For a day in the future when everything is shiny and bright

isn't that my birth right?

I remind myself of how far I've come

sometimes this soothes me some

Metamorphosis Of A Misfit

This trial is painful as I feel cheated of payment for work I've already done
working hard and long and not being compensated, that's no fun!

A decision is being drawn out to see if they'll pay me
at this point I want to forget about the world, just lay back, sip my tea

Dream of another place and time
where I get paid to write a rhyme!

I can picture myself now in a hammock by the sea
waves crashing, my husband and pets with me

Such a wonderful feeling and such a pretty picture frame
I want to hold dear to that and create my future the same

I want to reach out to my higher self, the future me
that version, that sometimes I lose sight of and forget to see

Her beauty, her heart
I don't want us to be apart

I want to embrace her ways, her spirit and kind
I want to reach in and read her mind

I want to model my life on hers as that's what makes my spirit soar
I'm tired of this frazzled version that is such a bore

I know I'm capable and can take small steps to transform, sigh
from this constrictive caterpillar suit to a beautiful butterfly

Metamorphosis Of A Misfit

I look forward to decluttering, simplifying and adding color to my life
I look forward to simplicity, peace, joy and no strife!

I can create this wherever I am, whatever zone
It's a matter of recognizing this and realizing, I'm not alone

I have support and courage and the power to change
transform into whomever I want, it's not that strange!

When I take the time to reflect on the part of me that I most want to be
I see endless opportunity

What do you see reflected in the highest version of you?
do you see abundant opportunity too?

We all have trials, what matters is how we choose
do we strive for a win-win or a lose?

Like crashing waves, things happen in sets
there will always be change, will you have regrets?

Or will you learn to ride the ups and downs
dress up in ridiculously extravagant gowns

Whatever it takes to make you smile
stick with your dreams, go that extra mile

The choice is yours, the time, now
dig deep, you know how

Metamorphosis Of A Misfit

From one transformer to another one
let's go change the world and have fun

Let's start with that beauty in the mirror, you see
what a difference we can make, you and me

Set aside your judgement and fear
let's get out of here

Go to a place where we feel at home and secure
or venture off on a grand tour!

We're all different and transform, our own way
what small step can you take today?

Trials, trials everywhere
are you brave or paralyzed by fear

Set your course and let your odyssey begin
start by journeying within

From there make a plan, create a map
then let everything flow through a tap

That you can turn off or on, from hot to cold
take a risk, step out of your comfort, be bold

There will always be trials, as there are transformations
life's a journey, full of sensations

Metamorphosis Of A Misfit

Take a deep breath and dive in
search around and find your kin

Your tribe, your angel pose, your network
you may end up with an incredible perk

A benefit of feeling supported, loved and accepted
encouraged, lifted up and no longer rejected

Enjoy the journey my friend
many blessings and love I send

Reflection Questions

1. When you think of transformation in your life, what areas or situations do you think of? What is your most incredulous transformation so far?

   _____
   _____
   _____
   _____
   _____
   _____
   _____
   _____

2. What works for you when you're going through a 'trial' in your life? What assists you to get back on track?

   _____
   _____
   _____
   _____
   _____
   _____
   _____
   _____

3. How will your life change, when you transform into the person you TRULY want and dream to be?

   _____
   _____
   _____
   _____
   _____

4. With transformation comes shifts and changes, what will open up in your life, when a magnificent transformation occurs?

5. If you're assisting a young adult through a transformation in their life, what advice would you give them? What support would you gift them?

6. How is the advice you gave above, applicable to you? Who can provide you with the support you desire during your transformation?

7. What do you need to let go of, in order to allow transformation to occur? How will you know you're recalibrated?

Recalibration Reals

This was literally a dream I had! I woke and started putting my dream into action immediately. Though my schedule and life has put a pause button on activating the interviews regularly, I have 10 interviews on youtube and loved every minute of the process. I was privileged enough to interviewing amazing people and discussing REAL topics that are not always openly talked about. It's my dream to assist people to validate their lives and all they encompass. To breakdown stereotypes and have curious conversations to assist in lifting each of us higher. We all have a dark side and ups and downs in life. Recalibration Reals is a celebration of ALL the ins and outs of our lives and capturing this on video, to share with the world.

Metamorphosis Of A Misfit

Recalibration Reals came to me in a dream
I woke with a vision seen

Of doing video interviews with people who inspire
people who never tire

Of living their dreams and using their super power
to make a higher

Impact in this universe
getting back up if they feel a curse

Of life throwing a curve ball or ten
struggling with balancing hardship and zen

Having real conversations to shine a light
on what it takes to make your plight

Make it yours and get up when you fall
you make the call

It's easy to feel down and out
beaten and wanting to shout

That life's not fair
you didn't get your share

Of what you deserve
feeling like you had to swerve

Metamorphosis Of A Misfit

To overcome disaster
feeling like your body's immobilized in plaster

The difficulty is in resilience and recalibration
turning failure into celebration

Learning and practicing ways
to make sure your not stuck in a haze

Of pity parties for too long
building resilience makes you strong

In my dream I saw interviews that exuded fun
little editing ever done

Real conversations with phenomenal human peeps
taking super hero leaps

Taking a passion and customizing it to fit
lighting a flame and keeping it lit

Reminding ourselves of who we aspire to be
we can see

Others who've blazed the trail
inspiring us to dust of after a fail

Often it's not learning something new
it's being reminded of how we flew

Metamorphosis Of A Misfit

Soared in the past
until a shadow was cast

Covering up and losing sight
of what once gave us flight

Enabling us to be invincible
living a life full

Recalibration Reals was a desire to kindle dreams
to believe you are capable, with the right teams

Frequently we make assumptions about a hero or heroine
do we really know where they've been?

What their life experience and journey entails
their fears and share of fails

We assume they are up here and we are there
we may assume they don't care

About helping someone they've never met
until we take the time, these assumptions are not set

In stone as truth
so take a seat in a comfortable booth

Watch a Recalibration Real
how does it make you feel?

Metamorphosis Of A Misfit

Everyone who WANTS to, can recalibrate
it's not only fate

That dictates your destiny today
you can shift things to go your way

How amazing reminding yourself, you can be different in just five
imagine that, take a dive

Into the infinite world of possibilities
release your sensibilities

Let your imagination run wild
release your inner most child

What are you capable of when recalibrated
how will you be satiated

Whatever lights your fire brightest
what ever you hold tightest

To your heart
set yourself apart

Make a mark
get through the dark

Into the light when you see yourself shine
participate in a deep mine

Metamorphosis Of A Misfit

Of digging around in your body, mind, and soul
releasing what takes a toll

Discovering extraordinary treasured delights
see and feel the sights

Dig deep and ask what is there to reveal
this is a huge deal

Sometimes we forget to frame the question right
we take flight

Without participating in the final check
what the heck!

This can lead to trouble with a capital T
do you see?

Ask your self over, and in a different way
listen close, to what you say

Recalibrate your state
make your life supernaturally great!

Metamorphosis Of A Misfit

Reflection Questions

1. Who do you admire as a role model? What will you look for in a role model to assist you to where you want to be?

   _____
   _____
   _____
   _____
   _____
   _____
   _____
   _____

2. What characteristics do these people have that you admire?

   _____
   _____
   _____
   _____
   _____
   _____
   _____
   _____

3. What will you recalibrate in your life, to allow your dreams to occur?

   _____
   _____
   _____
   _____
   _____
   _____
   _____
   _____

4. You're not the same person you were 5, 15 or 50 minutes ago, if you choose to change. Knowing you have the power to choose a different path or way of thinking in your life, how does this feel?

___

5. Knowing you have the choice to make a change and take a chance, what will you choose to shift?

___

6. How will your life be different when you create a mindset, allowing you to shine bright?

___

7. When you recalibrate your state, anythings possible. The more you practice creating a mindset that serves you best, the more capable you become to achieve your goals. In an ideal, fantastical world, what do you wish your thoughts would tell you? What will you love for your mind to believe?

-Treks Tracks & Travels-

Same Same But Different

This poem is a mish-mash of my world travels, racism, President Trump being elected in the USA and the Black Lives Matter movement. I was creating a piece of poetry to take to the National Speakers Association as I wanted to take a step out of my comfort zone and get some feedback. I was the only female in a room of 10 and what I hadn't realized was, this experience was a panel of four people analyzing, critiquing speakers for ten minutes. To say my poem didn't go over well is an under statement! One 'judge' murmured something about a high school poem, another told me I had to be careful of political implications and they didn't know where this would fit, in the corporate world. I was given some good technical advice about how to electronically display the poem, so I wasn't flicking through pages on a music stand and one judge said he loved poetry and enjoyed my reading. I left the academy session feeling deflated, humiliated (this is due to my sensitive nature, not anything anyone explicitly did to me!) and I wanted to hide under a rock and never come out. They had reflected back to me, my deepest fears; I wasn't good enough, an amateur at best and I would never get paid for doing what I loved most. OUCH!! After some comfort from friends and a pity party, I decided to keep doing what I'm doing and find a way to make it work. These men (apart from the one who liked poems) were not my ideal or target audience and I think I confused them because I didn't fit into a neatly marketable box. I felt confused about my place in the speaking world and I'm still figuring this out on my journey forward. I'm not sure who I'm writing for, or how to package my poems to make a living. For now, I know there are a few people who love my work and for them, I push through the discomfort of being an introvert, vulnerable and scared of not finding a tribe that I belong to.

Metamorphosis Of A Misfit

Do you look at me
and wonder what you see?

Do I look like you?
can you relate to what I do?

Do you think you know my story and soul?
where I've been - my life's toll

Why do we need to see a reflection
to see a glimmer of perceived perfection?

What assumptions do we make
when we have that first take?

When someone new approaches near
what runs through our brain to incite fear?

Why are we racist in our core?
like a cantankerous sore

Left untreated this can be a nasty deal
unconscious in its attempt to heal

Is it our culture, the way we were raised?
is it our lack of love and praise?

One thing I've noticed from traveling world wide
there's always an explanation for taking a side

Metamorphosis Of A Misfit

In Thailand I fell asleep under a coconut tree
I was awoken by a frantic local shaking me

He was old, with skin like dark leather
his face had seen its share of weather

I awoke with a start
not knowing this man's heart

He explained in broken English
that he found a wallet with a fish

I recognized the aqua wallet with its fish in pink
What does this man think?

Does he know he saved my life
stopped me from climbing a mountain of strife

I thanked him best I could, in broken Thai
opened the wallet and saw the baht inside

I offered him treasure, the little I had
of which he would not take and I felt sad

With his small frame standing tall
I realized I could repay him at his market stall

I was in need of a hat
I saw two, similar, both with ears like a cat

Metamorphosis Of A Misfit

I asked my new friend, "Why is this one 50 more cent?"
He laughed and said "same same but diff-er-ent!"

I laughed along not knowing the joke was on me
for it opened my eyes to what the world could be

I was looking for a bargain an explanation
what I received was a demonstration

That words and culture are not the reason
and the power of a smile can change a season

I didn't understand exactly what was meant
yet that toothless smile was worth the extra cent

His happiness with having not very much
was humbling and my heart it did touch

Australian culture is far from perfectly embracing
it would send my heart racing

Indigenous people or those from another land
were treated with distain, hate and a mean hand

I thought of that man and is generous grin
I thought of what and where he'd been

An easy life was certainly not, his past
yet he chose a wise net of love to cast

Metamorphosis Of A Misfit

He had no way to know of my deal in life
He treated me with kindness, there was no strife

I wondered why, the culture I grew up in
despite being blessed had darkness and sin

Sin in the sense of being mean spirited and cruel
killing ones hope with a brush of a tool

Some countries I visited had more, some had less
I wanted to get to the bottom of this mess

I moved to America seeing similar patterns of hurt
hearing of people saddened and pushed to the dirt

I wanted to look through childlike eyes
to see the world with glee and surprise

I thought of "same but different" over and again
then picked up my pen

I wrote similarities some of us are lucky to posses
I felt joy, peace and a soft caress

Of hope, alignment
visions of a new assignment

Similarities may appear different in color and form
there may be anomalies in abilities and 'norm'

Metamorphosis Of A Misfit

Yet on some level we are all "the same same"
we have the power to release the blame

What if we focused on HOW over WHY
ask ourselves what will make our spirits fly

What comes up when we think of HOW
can we make a difference NOW?

How can we do a random act?
how can we make a unique pact?

To be consciously aware
to unashamedly share

To brighten someone else's day
no matter who they are or what they say

How can we bridge the gap from different to same
how can we smile and re-frame

Our beliefs of what's true
to see something fresh & new

How can we make a new friend
how can we make amend

In my brain I imagine a world of magical hats
maybe the hats were decorated with cats!

Metamorphosis Of A Misfit

Maybe the hats were different colors and shapes
maybe they came with super powered capes!

The power of the magical hat
is to remind us of just that

Hats are as different and versatile as we are
serving different purposes, that are near and far

They are magical and serious, bright and defining
yet also "same same" and we all need reminding

That not everyone is the hat they wear
take time to listen and share

So every time you see someone new
this is what I ask of you

Be curious about their story book
use fresh eyes, take a different look

For until you've walked in their shoes
a judgment is not yours to use

Ask yourself HOW can I create a friendship united
be, less, short sighted

Maybe it's a gesture like a genuine compliment
you don't know its power, it may be heaven sent

Metamorphosis Of A Misfit

When you lay at night in your bed
you want a clear calm head

You want your magical night hat to shine bright
knowing you've made a difference and added light

To someone's life, you gave a gift
you used love to heal a rift

We all wear different hats journeying in this land
how will you use yours to lend a helping hand?

How will you use your magical talent
to change someone's day and be gallant

I wish you and your many hats a wondrous day
I challenge you to take away

One little message or tidbit of truth
so united we can act as a sleuth

Together we can make a difference to human kind
we can free our eyes from being blind

May you experience belonging in your heart
may love always be part

Of what you do and where you go
the influence of your actions, you may never know

Metamorphosis Of A Misfit

Forgiveness and a loving heart
will always set you apart

Please look into an-others eyes
look through their veiled disguise

Be curious, open hearted and kind
you may be blown away by what you find

We are all "same same but different" in some way
I hope this poem has changed your day

I hope with all my essence and being
that you embrace diversity and stay open to seeing

Where you can make a difference in someone's day
maybe change their luck in a miraculous way

Maybe offering a smile and hospitality
will be a way to set you free

It brings tears to my eyes, the magnificent kindness around
I've seen in my travels the brilliance of beauty abound

Thanks for your time, acceptance and grace
together we can positively influence the human race

Metamorphosis Of A Misfit

Reflection Questions

1. What's your favorite place that you've traveled to and why?

   _____
   _____
   _____
   _____
   _____
   _____
   _____

2. What's different about this place, when comparing it to where you live?

   _____
   _____
   _____
   _____
   _____
   _____
   _____

3. Where would you love to travel to?

   _____
   _____
   _____
   _____
   _____
   _____
   _____

4. Do you have any friends that are different from you culturally or politically? What is it that makes you friends?

_____
_____
_____
_____
_____
_____
_____
_____

5. What are things you're grateful for, that you were born with? This may be a skin color, religion, finance, family, gender, country, or freedom to have choice in your life._____

_____
_____
_____
_____
_____
_____
_____

6. What can you do - to contribute to a minority group where you live or world wide?

_____
_____
_____
_____
_____
_____
_____
_____

7. How would your life be different, if you were born into a different culture? What are the positives and negatives for you?

Am I There Yet?

I was annoying myself one day, by asking the question. You know the one - the really annoying question of 'are we there yet?' The way I was asking myself was in a high pitched tired wining voice of a 5 year old, sick of being on a road trip and not reaching their destination. I was feeling like maybe I had taken too many wrong turns and maybe, just maybe, I was beyond finding my way. I wondered if there was a certain allocation of wrong turns in ones life and if I'd used all mine! I was frustrated and wanted to know when I'd arrive. When would I feel like my life had worked. When would I feel happy and successful. When would my struggles, sweat and tears pay off. I wanted to know if I was getting close, if I would ever make it and how far off I was. I knew there was no black and white answer, yet still I probed to find some sort of relief, sign or guidance that my life was on track. I wanted proof that my life had purpose and meaning and that I was headed in the right direction for what I was put on this earth to do. Looking back now, with a baby girl added to our life and stumbling through a cancer diagnosis, this question almost takes on a different vibe. When I ask myself this question now - I feel strongly, powerfully and confidently that the answer is NO. I say this with a smile on my face, as I don't want to be there until my final day on this earth. I want to be a life long learner, experiencer and discover-er. I want to spread my wings far and wide and never be THERE until the end. '*There*' is constantly shifting, moving and adjusting. I don't have the same desire to answer this question, as I feel a trust and knowing that my path is exactly where it's supposed to be and when I reach '*There*' I'll know without asking!

Metamorphosis Of A Misfit

Am I there yet?
how will I know, what will I get?

Are you there yet?
what are the guidelines you use to let. . .

Yourself know, you've made it
you did it, you reached the top, now you can sit. . .

Enjoy the view, relax, breathe it all in
how do you know, does it come from within?

Are there measures and graphs, statistics and charts
what are, the integral parts. . .

That you rely on to let yourself know
I made it, I did it, now I can take it slow

Chillax and feel secure inside
with the knowledge of making it, what a ride

Is money the only way to tell
what if I don't like that smell. . .

The stench of only one measure
I want so much more pleasure. . .

I want to know, there are a variety of ways
to let myself know that I've used my days. . .

Metamorphosis Of A Misfit

In a valuable way, insightful and soulful
what's my measure, my inspirational pull?

I wake each morning and the thing that motivates me
seems simple and wondrous and sets me free

It's part money, part love, part adventure, part freedom and more
it's the opportunity to open many a door

To have a conversation and inspire lives a many
so only measuring using a penny. . .

Doesn't seem sublime at all
more like a roadblock - a stall

De-motivator and bland
not at all what I had planned!

I want a measuring tool that has sparkles and color, lights and sound
it shines bright, is versatile, limits unbound

I want to measure my progress with intuition
I want to meditate and play with temptation

I want to look from many different angles and directions
not to get hung up on imperfections

I want to dance and feel free
that is the perfect measure for me

Metamorphosis Of A Misfit

It may not be scientific or sound
it makes by heart sing, this is what I've found

To be playful, open and curious
can be most beneficial and less serious

Does that mean it's of lesser value and inaccurate?
meditate on that as you sit

See what your heart presents to you
do any of us really have a clue?

Maybe everyone's idea of making it, is as different as dreams
maybe nothings as it seems

What if making it, is only a fraction of what our focus is on
what if there was so much more, then it's gone?

So I ask you, have you made it? How do you know?
what's your secret, how does life flow?

Are you happy, divine and free?
if not, what would allow you to be?

Breathe in, breathe out
what is it, you want to shout

What's your message to the world and those in it
do you want others to feel, they don't have a limit?

Metamorphosis Of A Misfit

That they're capable of anything at all
or maybe they're safe, supported and won't fall

Without a safety net to catch them and prevent serious harm
that life is a series of ups and downs and provides a soothing balm

When this is necessary and needed
opportunities are seeded

Waiting for the right time and place
to grow, provide shelter and be in the race

The race of life, of fulfillment and longing
time and effort, practice and belonging

It can take time and effort to make it in life
there may be joy, maybe strife

Pick up after you fall, over, over and over again
there is no failure, only feedback, it doesn't have to be a drain

So when you ask me 'how do you know, if you've made it'
this is what I'll say, 'I have an impressive magical kit. . .

Inside are the measures of my; life, time, energy and love from the heart
passion, lessons and the effect on clients who felt torn apart

When you look in my eyes what do you see
someone who's made it, or the essence, of me?

Metamorphosis Of A Misfit

Either way I think you know the answer, it changes day by day
ask me tomorrow and see what I say!

I tell you, I've shifted, changed and become closer in alignment
with what makes me shine and need glasses with tint

to protect my eyes from the brightest sun
and in that space I've created fun

Lightness a freedom and a divine sense of belonging
I now have direction, for that I'm sure, my words I can sing. . .

Whisper or shout
that for me, is what it's all about!

Find your own way to measure, a way that feels true
see how that works, for you

I wish you luck on your journey ahead
may your days be story worthy and at night, rest your head

May you wake in the morning with a smile so bright
that you're motivated to take the ride no matter the sight

May you be guided internally and shine from within
may you reach for the stars and let the universe in

Collect supportive people around you, to lift you up
may it look half full when you see your cup

Metamorphosis Of A Misfit

You'll know when you've made it, I see that in you
you have the tools and knowledge, the next step is DO

Good luck my friend on your odyssey
may it take you to incredulous places and set you free

Reflection Questions

1. What will you feel, when journeying in the right direction in your life?

2. What will you see that let's you know you are on track in your life?

3. What feelings will you have that allow you to recognize success?

4. What areas of your life are you off track with?

   _____
   _____
   _____
   _____
   _____
   _____
   _____
   _____

5. What areas of your life are on track?

   _____
   _____
   _____
   _____
   _____
   _____
   _____
   _____

6. What are your biggest hurdles to your success?

   _____
   _____
   _____
   _____
   _____
   _____
   _____
   _____
   _____

7. What steps can you take, to get closer in alignment, to where you want to be? How will you put these steps into actionable bites?

___

Rambling Rose

On a road trip to Chicago, with my friend Susan Young, we talked non stop! She was asking me questions about my life, assisting me to create a skeleton layout of this book. Susan came up with the name Metamorphosis Of A Misfit. I later added, Finding Your Truth & Tribe. Susan told me I reminded her of a rambling rose, and that should be a chapter in my book! I never thought it was that strange to travel as much as I have. I didn't realize that to many people, this was a huge endeavor. In New Zealand (where I was born and lived till I was 13) and Australia (where I lived from 13-37) overseas travel is pretty common and almost an expected rights of passage either before studies start or the gap between studying and working. These trips are commonly 6-12 months and people leave with; a backpack, shoe-sting budget, a wish, and a prayer. Travel shaped my life in so many ways, I know I would NOT be the same person without it. I'm so grateful, for the experiences I had and the people I met. My travel adventures flow into all areas of my life and although I now have; a divine husband, 1 small human of 14 months, a mortgage, 2 cats, 1 dog, I still feel the energy, freedom and sweet smell of travel adventures. They just take on a slightly different form!

Metamorphosis Of A Misfit

Rambling rose
no one knows

When and where you'll go to next
maybe something will catch your eye, a flyer or even a text

You'll pack up your backpack and follow an adventure trail
no matter where it is or what you do, there is no fail

Lessons I've learnt, people I met
roads I traveled, no schedule set. . .

Cultures the scents, the foods and the smiles
I know it was worth traveling those miles

Your soul is at ease in foreign lands
feet so happy buried in the sands. . .

Sand on beaches
or even in water with leeches!

You've seen a lot and lived to tell the tale
from South America and the Inca trail

to Amsterdam, Australia and New Zealand
Italy, England, Denmark and Switzerland

Scenes exquisite and the people a delight
experiences that took your breath away, what a sight

Metamorphosis Of A Misfit

Cultures that seemed like they jumped out of a picture book
so surreal and magic, many photos you took

Friends you met that still to this day
you've kept in touch and continue to say

You'll always remember the odyssey you shared
that changed your life and directions were steered

Travel made you who you are today
it changed your life in such a way

You can barely imagine where you'd be without it
on a small farm in a one-horse town with a feeling like a pit. . .

A knot in your stomach, knowing there was more
you can sense it, it's so raw

Rambling Rose you'll always be
it's what makes your spirit free

Travel now modified and not as frequent
yet you still stir with the blow of the wind and smell of flint. . .

Igniting that travel spark
glowing so bright in the dark

Rambling Rose is in some, not all
large quantities, or maybe small

Metamorphosis Of A Misfit

It may look like a day trip or weekend get away
it may be a yearly travel plan to make you sway

And feel giddy with delight
and feel freedom at the sight

Of your ticket in hand
a trip you have planned

If you could go anywhere, where would it be?
who would you take and what sets your spirit free?

Maybe a spouse, kids or a lover
the world is a wonder and yours to discover

Rambling Rose small or large
travel wide, on plane or barge

Discover ways to explore new
maybe local, whatever suits you

Go, enjoy and be effervescent
see if it feels, heaven sent

Rambling Rose, feel in your heart
what is it, that sets you apart

Those content to stay in one place
I wonder what makes their heart race

Metamorphosis Of A Misfit

Rambling Rose, you may have many a thorn
you also have sweetness and beauty forlorn

Ever felt like following your gypsy spirit guide?
would she take you, far and wide?

Close your eyes and imagine now
where you'd go, will you even allow

Your mind to wander and dream
a waste it may seem

Yet I assure you it's not
play is essential, and all we've got

Left over from childhood and innocence so sweet
dream dreamers and follow your feet

Rambling Rose, I see you
for I am a gypsy, that at 13 flew

I knew at that time, the bug I'd caught
lands afar, are what I sought

Rambling Rose, set yourself free
so many choices and bountiful opportunity

Rambling Rose, I hear your call
trust and leap, you will not fall

Metamorphosis Of A Misfit

Fly with vigor
travel with rigor

This world and its people will make you shine bright as a star
for that's who you really are

From recycled stardust to human form
we're capable to weather many a storm

Rambling Rose, I feel your need
that spark, the ignition, the planning like a seed. . .

That will grow to fruition
with the right nutrition

Imagination and courage abound
your lost spirit will soon be found

Reflection Questions

1. Where was your last; trip, travel adventure, day excursion? What do you remember most about it?

   _____
   _____
   _____
   _____
   _____
   _____
   _____

2. If you could go anywhere you wanted, if money, time, and commitments were no problem, restriction, where would you go?

   _____
   _____
   _____
   _____
   _____
   _____
   _____

3. If you were to schedule a 30-60 minute DAY-SCAPE into your schedule (this may be self care, hike, driving somewhere awesome, exploring a new park, visiting a friend) how would that feel?

   _____
   _____

4. If you were to plan a yearly travel trip, where would you go? Who would go with you? How long would you be away? What experience will you get from this trip?

5. When you prioritize 'travel' whether it's 30 minutes or 30 days, how will that change your life from how it is now?

6. How will travel adventures (large or small) shape your life?

7. What gifts will you discover in your self and others?

-Introspection-

Versatile Vulnerability

I didn't realize I was being vulnerable in my coaching and presentations, until someone told me! I guess I assumed that everyone spoke their truth, even shared the messy bits. I then read Brene Brown's book The Gifts of Imperfection and I realized that vulnerability came naturally to me, SOMETIMES. There are areas of my life, I'm working on being vulnerable and trusting. Speaking and coaching allow me to be vulnerable as I subconsciously know that it assist others. It gives them 'permission' to allow their stories to be told without shame. When I'm not on a stage or coaching, sometimes I struggle with being vulnerable. Today I'm in day 8/14 of using a chemotherapy topical cream (to treat skin cancer) on my face, it causes red blotches and at 42, I look like a hormonal teenager with a face full of acne! Talk about being vulnerable, I have to chat with myself (the conversation is tricking me into believing people wont think I have some sort of contagious disease!) before leaving the house. I second guess wether or not to go to the gym. I feel people staring and wondering. In these moments of feeling exposed and vulnerable, I remind myself of this little prayer 'feel the fear and let love near.' this reminds me to tap into the universal powers of love, to remind myself of my husband, my daughter, friends and family who love me, this gives me strength.

Metamorphosis Of A Misfit

Vulnerability I found out
makes people want to shout

They even laugh at your pain
not in a mean way, that would be insane

More like in a funniest home videos type of way
you laugh at someone's mishaps because you too have had to pay

The price of hurt and looking foolish and ashamed
who was it that you blamed?

Maybe someone assisted your vulnerability feelings or hurt
maybe you wanted to rub their face in the dirt?

Or maybe you fessed up to the whole situation being your fault
either way, vulnerability is like a vault

It contains hidden treasures and jewels that are rare
ever captivate an audience and have them stare

At you and through you and then you saw the mark and their gentle pace
the glistening mark of a tear trickling down their face

In that instant you knew that others could relate
you weren't alone with your fate

Vulnerability allows a connection that is beautiful and unique
people open up to you as they hear you speak

Metamorphosis Of A Misfit

Your words, seemingly right, just for their ears
allowing them to let go and release fears

When someone is vulnerable you feel a connection
something heartfelt, a deep section

Of you relating to them, by an invisible thread
they had the courage to share and get inside your head

Vulnerability can heal the deepest wound or make you howl at the moon
mend a broken heart and make you swoon

There is an essence of grace
feeling you are not alone in the human race

Brene Brown the goddess of vulnerability study
lets us know through research that we all need a buddy

Someone we feel connected to, safe, loved and secure
this assists us to move forward like a lure

Tempting us to be brave and do, do, DO again
it is only then

We can pick ourselves up and start to heal
feeling supported and fulfilled like a nourishing meal

A meal of food, spirit and courage
a beloved security allowing us to release our baggage

Metamorphosis Of A Misfit

It's reassuring that we're all in this together
comfort in numbers, birds of the same feather

In our society vulnerability is not always embraced
maybe because we are always in such haste

To get ahead
build big, then we're dead

We forget to really live life
we focus so much on strife

We forget to smell the earth and all it has to offer
we didn't dig deep, this causes us to suffer

What will happen if you're vulnerable today?
who might you inspire, in a deep and meaningful way?

A family member, a friend or stranger in need
that would be amazing indeed

Take a deep breath in and slowly release air through your teeth
let go of any fears you have, about what's underneath

Stand up tall and take a stance
to be vulnerable and dance

Like no one's watching, you're free as a bird
does this sound healing or absurd?

Metamorphosis Of A Misfit

If somethings not working in your life
do something different and cause less strife

Give it a go and see what happens to you
it may be magical, I appreciate what you do

Live a life of extreme divinity
life is short, for that is a certainty

So let go of your tense shoulders, strict rules & self-imposed lies
dive into vulnerability and see where your body and mind flies

Take note of the location and feeling
you don't need to stay stuck under a glass ceiling

You have lessons for others in this life time
in your own unique way, not necessarily in rhyme!

How can your vulnerability save another life
maybe a mother, a lover or wife

Maybe in a small tiny way
you can be set free and have your say

Feel heard, honored and secure
knowing your heart is pure

In its intentions to let others know
you can move fast or slow

Metamorphosis Of A Misfit

It's not the timing, it's the momentum in the race
that can take you, to an amazing place

My vulnerability may be your release
so on this day may you feel peace

Rest easy knowing you're not alone
sit in your chair, like it's a throne

For you are a VIP
trust your heart, you'll see

Trust, listen and take time
to feel rhythm and rhyme

Even if you march to a different beat
you still deserve the very best seat

The one that's unique to you
the one with the most amazing view

Sit on your seat in nature or a room
and know you are loved, supported and soon

You'll feel the power and strength inside
to live your life with passion and pride

This life is a roller coaster adventure
remember to come back to your center

Metamorphosis Of A Misfit

We're all vulnerable in different ways
choose the best fit for you and make your days. . .

Count and live fully and free
that's your birthright, the way it's meant to be

Reflection Questions

1. When was the last time you felt vulnerable?

   _____
   _____
   _____
   _____
   _____
   _____
   _____
   _____

2. Do you view vulnerability as a strength or weakness? Why?

   _____
   _____
   _____
   _____
   _____
   _____
   _____
   _____

3. How do you feel when someone shows you vulnerability?

   _____
   _____
   _____
   _____
   _____
   _____
   _____
   _____

4. What area of your life would you like to allow vulnerability? Why?

_____
_____
_____
_____
_____
_____
_____

5. How can you use your vulnerability to assist others?

_____
_____
_____
_____
_____
_____
_____

6. What scares you most about being vulnerable?

_____
_____
_____
_____
_____
_____
_____

7. If you allowed your vulnerability, how would your life be different? Who in your life would be most affected by this?

Bio-Individual Bravery

This poem was written when thinking about a conversation a friend and I had. She told me I was brave. Immediately I felt unworthy and wondered why she'd told me that. It wasn't that I thought she would tell me something, she did not believe. It was something I was unable to embrace, as I didn't see this element in my being. This conversation stayed with me and rattled around for days and weeks. When I put fingers on keyboard - this was the result! I allowed myself to recognize bravery in myself, in many ways I had not imagined before. I discovered there are so many acts of bravery that most of us perform on a daily basis. We all have bio-Individuality, we are all unique, so it makes sense that our acts of bravery differ! The more we support each other, recognize, and acknowledge acts of bravery within us, the more a ripple effect will occur. Imagine if people in our community, country and world felt brave. If there was a sense of accomplishment within our lives. It's so easy to get caught in comparison traps and forget how far we've come in this lifetime. Taking time and effort to celebrate achievements, no matter how small - can have a massive impact over time.

Metamorphosis Of A Misfit

What is bravery and who has it?
do you think of soldiers, saviors or a bandit?

Is it a child who survives cancer?
or a mother who's a dancer?

Is it you?
who knew!

We may associate bravery with grandeur and size
yet there are moments small and with no lies

That are also brave
to whisper and inspire or rant and rave

the choices we make can ultimately be heroic
maybe graceful, maybe stoic

I felt scared when I fell off my horse
brave when I got back on of course!

I felt scared when I read my first a speech at 13
brave when years later I did it again

I was terrified when going on my first date
brave when it turned out first rate!

I was heartbroken about ending a relationship I was in for 5 years
brave when I recognized it was not nourishing me, causing pain and tears

Metamorphosis Of A Misfit

I was almost paralyzed in fear of my first overseas travel solo
brave when I practiced relaxing and going with the flow

Excited and fearful of moving out at 17
brave when I experienced freedom and creating a beautiful scene

Decisions feeling crippling and confusing
I felt brave when I took a stand and saw them more as amusing!

I felt scared to stand up to a person hurting my friend
I felt brave and proud to assist them and see the hurt mend

I took a risk when moving to the USA
now look, I'm still here today!

I was nervous as hell when reconnecting with Cris
it had been 10 years since we'd seen each other, now I'm Mrs instead of Miss

There were many tears and near quitting with my business venture
I feel brave when now I see it as my best ever adventure

We all have braveness in us and sometimes we forget
to take that leap and get a little wet

Take a chance and see what happens to you
practice, you'll create neural pathways too

These pathways will let your brain know, being brave is ok
you'll survive and maybe plan a new life, today!

Metamorphosis Of A Misfit

You can reinvent yourself anytime you choose
bundle up your greatness, bravery and believe you can't lose

Then take a big leap to where you desire to go
maybe you will never know

What your true potential is unless your bravery gets a call to action, a shout
then you start to catch a glimpse of your greatness and realize it will all work out!

Like Dad told me "if you make a decision and its wrong (by a ton)
make another one!"

What are you capable of when you are feeling brave
who's life will you save?

Is it your own
will you see how much you've grown

In intellect, spirit and tenacity
you're more capable than you know, you'll see

Take your bravery, wrap it round you like a cloak
sprinkle it in your bath water when taking a soak

Eat it for breakfast, lunch and dinner
look in the mirror and see you're a winner!

For what is brave for one is not for another
maybe it's a fit for you and not your mother!

Metamorphosis Of A Misfit

Figure out how bravery can fit into your day
feel the fear and do it anyway

I see in you bravery, yes I do
so let it out, don't keep it trapped like bars in a zoo

Polish it up and set it free
let's see what version of you, you'll be

What do you want your tombstone to read?
stayed in the box of life OR lived with bravery and passion to be freed

It's your choice and who am I to be judge or jury
I was scared of my own shadow and filled with fury

For a life half lived was what I choose
until I broke that mold and struck a pose

Of strength and determination
now my life's a sensation!

Not every day, some are braver than others are
yet I'm proud to bear the scar

The mark of living life to the full
of sometimes running like a bull

Or making a spontaneous decision
to have an adventure instead of a collision

Metamorphosis Of A Misfit

Do you feel your bravery, can you look it in the eye?
we are one of the same you and I

We are humans in this world, we are opportunistic
be brave, seize the moment, despite seeming like a lunatic!

I've been told more than once by well-meaning friends and family
that maybe my head needs looking at, "do you have the insanity?"

They have positive intentions, I know they do
I don't wish the same restrictions for you

You are brave, I know it to be true
so get out there and let's see what you're capable to do

Metamorphosis Of A Misfit

Reflection Questions

1. Who do you know that is brave? What makes them brave?

   _____
   _____
   _____
   _____
   _____
   _____
   _____
   _____

2. If you were brave, what would you accomplish?

   _____
   _____
   _____
   _____
   _____
   _____
   _____
   _____

3. How would you describe bravery to a 5 year old?

   _____
   _____
   _____
   _____
   _____
   _____
   _____
   _____

4. In what areas are you uniquely brave?

_____
_____
_____
_____
_____
_____
_____

5. Knowing you are capable of change every day, what will you do this week that is BRAVE?

_____
_____
_____
_____
_____
_____
_____

6. How will you strengthen your bravery to allow it to grow stronger?

_____
_____
_____
_____
_____
_____
_____

7. How will others be influenced by your bravery?

Inner Wisdom

There are times in my life when I remember to check in with my inner wisdom and times I do not! When I lose sight of this magical gift, my life goes out of alignment. This poem was written in the first year of my business, when I was struggling to figure out which direction to go in and how to overcome obstacles. Hindsight is a wondrous thing and had you told me that this is what I would be speaking and coaching about, I'm not sure I would have believed you! I remember taking the time to intentionally go within and listen. It seemed like a long time since I had done this and the feeling was like coming home. A feeling of peace, gratefulness and calm. I remember feeling amazed at the insights revealed and then mystified as to why I didn't do this more! Where will your inner wisdom journey take you?

Metamorphosis Of A Misfit

Inner wisdom where do you hide
why can't I find you and where is my guide

I feel lost, useless and alone
I'm tired of hearing myself cry and moan

I'm a people pleaser, just tell me what to do
I'll do it eagerly, just for you

when it comes to myself, I have more doubt
I murmur, when I want to SHOUT!

I question each step I take, I'm grounded from flight
chastise myself when things don't go right

I see in others, what I wish I had
I'm glad for them yet still feel sad

There seems to be a disconnect between what I dream
and the means I have to access the right team

A team of support crew so encouraging and wise
nope, just me here bound by invisible ties

Doesn't feel safe to figure out what I really want to do
because "that's frivolous, wasteful and wouldn't be good for you"

I can hear the critic voice now
the gremlin brain attacking - POW!

Metamorphosis Of A Misfit

Henry Ford said "if you believe you can or believe you can't, either way your right
this intrigues me, I feel it and it's within my sight. . .

The courage to search deep inside
to hear the voice of criticism and let it slide

What if I trusted my inner wisdom, deep inside?
what if I just went for it and forgot about my pride?

What would arrive and how would I change?
how would I change others, strange

These questions of curiosity and intrigue
maybe this is the one to join, the "Wisdom League!"

So search I did, high and low
dove into books and many seeds did I sow

Not in that way
let's just say

I planted seeds of inspiration, courage and hope
I no longer felt useless and bound by a rope

I felt a glimmer of freedom, excitement and joy
like a little kid that has a new toy

I bounced around and skipped with glee
watch out world, there's no stopping me

Metamorphosis Of A Misfit

I asked questions that went deeper
what was revealed is that I wanted to be a speaker!

What would I have, to tell people about, what would I say?
why would they listen and really, they would pay?

This seemed slightly absurd yet curiously stirring
what else is inside me, lurking and luring?

Well it seems I would love to be an author too
interesting, I think I passed English with marks, just a few

Logic and inner wisdom seem conflicted
yet I know there's a way to feel less restricted

I'll meet the inspirational teachers when the time is right
I will hold this dream close and never lose sight

Of what I deeply desire and want to experience in this lifetime
I want to explode into color, and movement - not be a constricted mime

So inner wisdom has a special place in my heart
together we will always be, never apart

There will be times, I'll forget to search
then I'll hear from that bird on its little perch

The one on my shoulder, whispering for me to remember
you don't have to wait till December

Metamorphosis Of A Misfit

To receive gifts, sing songs and feel a happy vibe
trust your inner wisdom and use that as your guide

When was the last time you really searched, deep inside
shone a flashlight on all the dark places and went on a 'me ride'

It's a ride without a doubt
ins and outs, ups and downs, maybe a smile or shout!

It's a ride well worth the expense and may change your life
so live large and magnificent and release the strife

Believe in miracles and wonder and magical teas
know that you are full of boundless possibilities

Go within, alone or with a friend
see what old scars you'll mend

When you believe and trust
the doors of opportunity will open, they must

That's how things work, not always in ways or times we want them to
yet they will open just the same, providing insight for you

What will you do with your wisdom from within?
use it to illuminate your life? OR trash it, in a bin?

Choice is yours and yours alone
want to wake up in the morning with a sparkle or groan?

Metamorphosis Of A Misfit

The choice is yours and choose it you will
there are billions of ways to create a bill

Open your heart, body, spirit and mind
you may be overjoyed at what you find

Reflection Questions

1. In what voice does your inner wisdom speak?

2. Where are the best places for you, to get in touch with your inner wisdom?

3. When taking a journey inside of you, what do you need to pack? What do you need before or during your journey?

4. If your inner wisdom had three words to be inspire you, what would they be?

5. When in your life have you felt most inspired? What allowed this inspiration?

6. If you speak to the future you, five years from now, what wisdom will your future self tell you?

7. When you tap into your 'well of wisdom' how will this effect your life?

-Tribe-

Kool Kids Tribe

My two dear friends and I were sitting having coffee when this conversation happened. It basically started when one friend noticed, she was treated differently in a networking group to someone else who had been their longer and kind of in with the cool crowd. She jokingly said, 'why aren't we Cool Kids?' Keep in mind the age of this group of three peeps is around 40-60ish! We started laughing and decided that we were all Cool Kids in our own lunch boxes!!

We threw questions around to figure out how people in this group were the Kool Kids! We came up with things like; time people had been established with this organization, money or success they had with their business, tight friendship with others already established in the cool group and we couldn't quite pin point what made this group of 'cool kids' other than a click. We also noticed, there were a handful of people who would cross over from the cool kids group to the rest of us, kind of bridging the gap! It was like reliving high school, all over again, except a lot funnier! We decided to make our own Kool Kids group and do fun stuff and celebrate each other for our unique Kool-Ness-Is!

Metamorphosis Of A Misfit

Never been a Kool Kid in my life
caused to much strife

To figure it out and conform
I didn't want to be a norm

I wore strange clothing and rainbow boots
I never had lunch money and ate sandwiches and fruits

My clothes were from K Mart or second hand
I wasn't in demand

For being anyones friend
I tend

To be a loner
loving being a world roamer

Don't get me wrong, I love people a lot
just can't stand small talk and some of the rot

That comes out of peoples mouths and brain
it's insane

The magnitude of mean
I'd rather be unseen

I guess I was on the fringes of being normal
I didn't respect the formal

Metamorphosis Of A Misfit

Constructs of how to play the Kool Kids game
It's a shame

I didn't feel the comfort and power I feel now
of being a 'purple cow'

Seth Goden, wrote a book on it
what a perfect fit

For an outsider to see
that's what can set them free

Being different is more accepted now and also has a long way to go
I want you all to know

Despite what you may think
it does really stink

When you're excluded, made fun of, bullied and left out
there is no doubt

This has a lasting affect on your day to day
no matter what your age, you can still feel that way

You felt when you were young
I don't hold my tongue

Like I used to
I say what I feel if you

Metamorphosis Of A Misfit

Are being mean to someone or a group as a whole
your words and actions take a toll

So now as an adult in the fourth decade of my existence
I face some mental resistance

To make a conscious decision to be in with the crowd
or stay dreaming on my cloud

I'm mostly in my own little bubble
and I feel the rubble

Piling up as I climb the hill of being an entrepreneur solo
I get to choose who I follow

This is my code
to travel the road

Of the less explored and most curious
I would be remiss

If I didn't share it with you!
My choice is to hang out with people I love, there are a few

Super amazing humans that I just can't get enough of
they're my source of inspiration and love

They're the ones who lift me higher
who support my desire

Metamorphosis Of A Misfit

To live my life on my terms
to not worry to much about germs

To play and have adventures galore
to sometimes just roar

For no other reason than venting
frustrations of renting

Out my brain for earning money to survive
when I want to thrive

Creating what I love most
living in color not like a ghost

Barely there and scary
I want to be a freakin awesome fairy

Granting wishes to those who need them most
living on more than plain toast

Living a life that has sparkles and Disco Balls
glittering on the walls!

If you don't make me laugh out loud
if you don't make me feel proud

To be who I am, embracing my crazy
then our relationship at best will be hazy

Metamorphosis Of A Misfit

Let me tell you about two friends who're the best
Jacy and Mary Helen go above and beyond the test

Of what true friendship is
they effervescently fizz

They fill my cup
lift me up

Inspire me to be a better me
ground me when I want to flee

They gift me life when I feel depleted
they prevent me from staying unseated

They make me laugh and their smiles are a joy
there's no hidden agenda or ploy

I can tell you now that these two are the Koolest Kids ever
and I will never

Forget the way they treated me
when it would have been easy for them to see

That I was slightly unstable
like a three legged table

I had health issues and cancer
I'm not a great dancer

Metamorphosis Of A Misfit

At times I was just a big mess
yet they would guess

And find ways to make me better
Kooler Kids - well I never

Found any like these two gals
we are a trio of pals

That are cool to the core
yet warm to the touch and not a bore

You may hear us laughing across the street
it's hard to beat

That soul nourishing mix
of friends that fix

Everything wrong
and remind you to sing a song

Because 'when you sing, you can't cry'
I think of my friends words often and sigh

As she helps me through another time
of feeling less than sublime

Pick your Kool Kids Tribe with care
as precious jewels are rare

Reflection Questions

1. Have you been a Kool Kid? If you have or have not - how was the experience for you?

2. How do you know if you're in the cool crowd or not?

3. If you were to create your own Kool Kids Tribe, what will the guidelines be and who do you know that you would LOVE to invite to your group? Your invitees may be actual people you know or famous people/mentors/inspirers that you think would be phenomenal additions to your group.

_____
_____
_____

4. When you imagine your Kool Kids Tribe, what will be your vibe, your mission, feeling within the group?

_____
_____
_____
_____
_____
_____
_____
_____

5. What will happen when you create this group? Maybe it's; mastermind mentors, book club, networking tribe, philanthropy posse, whatever it is, how will this be a greater good in the world?

_____
_____
_____
_____
_____
_____
_____
_____

6. What is the first step toward creating an awesome tribe of Kool Kids?

_____
_____
_____

7. Knowing what you now know and reflecting on life experiences, what will you share with the part of your self that's felt left out or treated as less than?

Trust & Adjust

I was in a mastermind group that Sheri Maass created. It was a fabulous group of women entrepreneurs that assisted me greatly on my solo-preneur journey. One morning one of the women asked this question "How do you know when to make a decision?" There were many answers and I listened deeply, taking in the generous advice. Out of no where, I blurted out "trust and adjust!" After the words left my mouth, I elaborated on what the words meant for me and how they can stop you from staying stuck. My Dad told me that if I made a decision and it was the 'wrong one' I always had the power to make another one. This helped me so many times throughout my life and I think my trust and adjust is derived from the essence of Dad's wisdom. There were times in my life that I literally felt paralyzed with fear of making a decision and would drive myself (and those around me) crazy with procrastination. The result was deep frustration and stuck-ness. When I embraced and practiced making a decision, momentum took hold and life was more fluid and fun!

Metamorphosis Of A Misfit

A mastermind of women posed a question to the group
I answered with a verbal soup

Then what came to me were 3 simple words
"Trust and Adjust" flying like a bird

A bird with a message that first you trust
then you make changes to adjust

This works for goals and life
set your sights then change if strife

This means that life happens as it will
change is inevitable and there's no magic pill

Trust you made a decision for the right reason
and adjust with a change in season

Decisions are made with education & knowledge at a particular stage
this is developmental and unless you're a Sage

There's no way to predict with certainty and a prayer
so take a leap and stand clear

See what happens, experience and ask 'how does this feel?'
adapt and adjust as you see real

At different stages in our timeline
we prioritize accordingly, you have yours & I have mine

Metamorphosis Of A Misfit

When you feel paralyzed by taking a chance
remember to have fun and prance!

Life is not forever and neither are your decisions
you may have some rough collisions

Better to be participating in life
than incapacitated with strife

Figure out what it is you desire
know you can't control exactly when you retire

Then trust
feel lust

The passion in your day
sculpting your life in a magical way

Adjust as the wind changes it's course
reposition like riding a horse

Review your situation and see with new eyes
release the should's and binding ties

Trust and adjust - living life to the full
take charge and run like the bull

Fierce and strong
knowing you can do no wrong

Metamorphosis Of A Misfit

It may seem there are a million reasons why
you should clip your wings and not fly

Millions of reasons and people too
who are affected by your decision new

I ask you "will these people be affected by you NOT living your dream?"
all is not always as it may seem

Life is often too short
to be trapped within a rectangular court

Think bigger, brighter, bolder and blue
or whatever color is most suited to you

The ocean colors are my favorite
draped in these fabrics I sit

Smiling at the delight of my trust
knowing at any stage I can adjust

It's a permission slip to give you a green light
giving you intuitive sight

Reminding you of what you already know
all that's left to do is GO!

Wherever that may be
follow your heart and flee

Metamorphosis Of A Misfit

Fly to where your spirits soar
there's no need to compromise till you are raw

Make a plan
knowing you can

Accomplish anything you're inspired to do
what is the magnificent you

Waiting for?
the right time or lore

I have news for you my friend
your heart will never mend. . .

If you wait for everything to be in perfect alignment
sometimes gifts are heaven sent

You can choose to trust
this is a must

To propel you forward into extraordinary heights
setting your sights

Thousands of times higher than you ever dreamed possibly true
believe it my friend, for it's you

You are more capable, than you may know
every day you may choose to grow

Metamorphosis Of A Misfit

Closer to your goals
closer to those souls

That'll support, encourage, inspire and lift you up
filling your phenomenal cup

The choice is yours for the taking
mixing and baking

Adding in ingredients that you love and adore
adjusting amounts in case you want more

Trust and adjust, it may set you free
bring you back to who you were born to be

Trust and adjust, let go
what seeds will you grow?

Trust and adjust, you can do no wrong
life is like your favorite song

There will always be a twist and turn
allowing you to learn

To lean closer to what it is you really desire
to set you free to climb higher

I'm excited to see and hear of your odyssey
trust and adjust, set your spirit free

Metamorphosis Of A Misfit

Reflection Questions

1. What's a decision you would love to have clarity around? You would love to have guidance on which choice to make.

   _____
   _____
   _____
   _____
   _____
   _____
   _____

2. What would happen if you flipped a coin to make this decision? Why would you follow or not follow, what the coin dictated?

   _____
   _____
   _____
   _____
   _____
   _____
   _____

3. Who else is affected by this decision?

   _____
   _____
   _____
   _____
   _____
   _____

4. How will it feel to make an educated, heartfelt decision on the facts and feelings you have at this present time - knowing you can make an adjustment if needed?

5. What needs to be in place, in order for you to feel safe in making this decision?

6. How will you know you've made the right decision?

7. What's the cost to you, of NOT making a decision and staying in a place of stuckness?

What's Possible Now?

This poem was inspired after I recorded a Recalibration Reals interview with Kim Kotecki. She was telling me about their basement flooding and their immediate reaction was fear and despair. Then they remembered their friend's advice, his fabulous question "what's possible now?" They looked through different eyes and started to think of all the fun, interesting, amazing things they could do with their basement. Let me tell you, the Kotecki basement ROCKS! It's beautiful and filled with love, Jason's creative art work and incredible office and art space. I love this question as a tool to use throughout life. It's a reminder that disasters can be recalibrated into opportunities of a lifetime!

The modality I use in coaching is NLP (neuro-linguistic programming) and Kim's "What's possible now" reminded me of an NLP question that asks "what if. . .?" This question allows people to break out of the mental path they are on and see their surroundings in a new way. Questions are so powerful and can literally change and shift you life. There are a million different possibilities on the best way to live your life and YOU get to choose the path you'll explore. YOU get to choose how you'll navigate the ups and downs of life and the direction you'll go in. That's powerful stuff!

Metamorphosis Of A Misfit

My friend Tofe Evans wrote a book called *Everyone Has a Plan Till SH*%* Hits The Fan*

This made me laugh so much and you know it's true!
what's ever gone wrong for you?

When sh*% hits the fan
what's your go to plan?

Do your bury your head and pretend it's not there
do you leave to escape the fear

What are the tools you have in place
what allows you to deal, with grace?

What's possible now is a powerful thing to ask
it can be a monumental task

To piece your life back together
breaking fee from the despair teether

What if, things are more than what they seem
what if, there's a way to make a magnificent team

A tribe of like minded souls
all working together to reach their goals

Anything and everything is possible when you choose to see
past the borders and desire to flee

Metamorphosis Of A Misfit

When you look with new eyes and imagine magic
this can be possible from something tragic

Take my best friend dying of Hodgkinsons Disease
I would've done anything to put her at ease

Yet through her passing the unfathomable came true
I was reconnected with Cris - I'm telling you

Without Kat's death, I may never have reconnected with this amazing man
the father of our sweet baby, the love of my life, my number one fan

What about when I left teaching due to a breakdown and bullying?
it allowed an opportunity to recalibrate and keep moving

Yes it was painful and a financial mess
yet without that push, I'd be stuck in a life of stress

Yes I had to redefine who I was, my purpose
it was worth it, the struggle to experience that sweet kiss

This kiss that life gives you when you're following your life part
the kiss from you lover that melts your heart

So I ask myself what if this situation is a blessing
what if everything is worth readdressing

What if this is the best thing that's ever gone down
what if now, I get to wear a crown!

Metamorphosis Of A Misfit

What's possible now with this new disaster
I can use plaster

To sculpt a new life, a new opportunity, a new me
just the way I want my life to be

What if this was a gift in disguise
what if it's a turning point to embrace the wise

Part of me that was scared to shine
maybe this disaster is fine!

What's possible now in this place of despair
how can I assist others, now I'm down here?

What if, it was all meant to be
so cliche and now I see

The meaning behind these fickle words of few
there is a master plan for me and for you

There are people who take adversity
they shake it up and alchemize it into a university

A learning establishment where they enter as this green type
metamorphosing into a fruit so ripe

Experience, education, life experience and culture
mould us into a particular sculpture

Metamorphosis Of A Misfit

What if you were to get some tools
chip away the fools

Design, shift and change
embody the strange

Uncomfortableness of the unknown
look at the seeds you've sown

What you water grows
look where your energy flows

What's possible now, in your life story?
anything you want, unique glory

Is at your fingertips for you to grab
shift your vision and see your slab

Of moulding clay
as more than dull grey

That slab of clay is a magical form, waiting for your construction
or leading you to a path of despair and destruction

What will you choose?
what've you got to loose?

In looking at the sunny side of life and imagining the best
life is like a litmus test

Metamorphosis Of A Misfit

Imagine you have the power to transform heartache to glee
you have the power to be all you can be

What"s possible now is freedom for you
to do

Whatever it is that'll make your heart shine
be sublime

Live every day as if it mattered
feel your worries scattered

In the wind like dandelion pieces
floating gracefully across the beaches

What if you life was majestic
you get to pick

How you create your highest purpose, roll, rock and live
you choose to whom you give

What's possible now is you get to choose
you'll never lose

As long as you recalibrate
imagine and calculate

Your life will be first rate
you'll open the golden gate

Metamorphosis Of A Misfit

What if you're more capable than you know
what if from this experience you'll grow

Into the most phenomenal human you ever dreamed up
your mindset like a half full cup

Looking on the bright-side and embracing the positive
freedom to choose to whom you give

This life is an incredible gift
it's up to you to sift

The crap from the jewels
be you and use all the tools

Accessible to you to craft a life you love
RISE ABOVE

Reflection Questions

1. What's the worst thing that's happened to you recently?

2. How did you deal with it? How effective was that for you?

3. When disaster strikes, how long do you allow yourself to stay in a place of stuck?

4. Who or what is your best resource of moving your state of mind when it seems immovable?

___

5. What's possible now in your life?

___

6. What are your roadblocks; blocking your way to awesomeness, achieving your goals and living your most awesome life?

___

7. What if you were coached and those roadblocks were transformed into stepping stones? What are you capable of with 100% support, encouragement and believe in your quest in life?

___

-Desired State-

Continental Confidence

This poems name came from a Key & Peel skit (based on a Continental Breakfast) that made me laugh at how much enjoyment the character was having with his meal, provided by the hotel. It was funny on the level of enjoyment of the simple things as well as turning something that is generally viewed as normal or ordinary into an extraordinary adventure. I was amazed going through my poems, how many I had written about ONE corporation and a negative experience I had there. I'd forgotten over time, how devastating this experience was. Reflecting now, I feel a little embarrassed by the whole situation and wonder how I let it get under my skin. At the same time, I acknowledge my pain during this experience and offer my past self, a big hug and a reminder of how far I've come. Writing poems is a way for me to deal with issues that seem impossible to solve. When I feel so stuck, and I don't know which way to turn, it's like the words shine a light on my darkness and releases, the grip of despair.

Metamorphosis Of A Misfit

Confidence on the go
where it ends up, only you know!

Sometimes it's there sometimes it's not
when it's there you can fly sky high, see earth as a dot

Your spirits soar and you're invincible and free
that's the way I want to be

Right now my confidence has dipped into the empty sign
it's been a while since it's been this low and on the decline

I feel sad, I'm trapped in a mindset that's effecting my life
the decisions I'm not making, are causing strife

This happened over just a few weeks
it's unbelievable that just a few tweaks

Of one person in one corporation and I'm a mess
what this person did was unethical, it still effects me nonetheless

I feel shattered, worthless, trapped and depressed
it takes effort and motivation, just to get dressed

Over and over again, trouble was brewing
more than once, I thought of suing

I knew I was in the right
and deep down, I realized this wouldn't help my plight

Metamorphosis Of A Misfit

This episode of work was done
I wish I could celebrate and have fun

That's part of the problem, the corporation owed me a month's pay
I still clearly remember the day

I received the e mail saying they would offer me a pittance of what I was worth
it cut like a knife and threw me to the earth

Intuitively I knew this corporation and I, would part ways
I assumed we would have about 200 more days!

As best laid plans can often do
when things happen to me and you. . .

That we're not necessarily expecting or prepared for
feel like I'm becoming a bore

My focus is narrow and limited beliefs are running wild
feel like an insecure, sullen child

Yesterday was the turning point for me
an event occurred that set me free

I felt so low and miserable, a decision had to be made
the deadline was approaching and a payment was due to be paid

This is a yearly event that for me was so enticing
in the state I was in, I was paralyzed by the expensive pricing

Metamorphosis Of A Misfit

it was out of my range, I told myself with a tear in my eye
I'm not worth it, my critter brain would cry

I slept on this, being miserable all day
the following morning, I remembered what I'd say

How I'd talk to myself when confidence was one of my friends
surely there was a way, to make amends

I remember making an investment of $6000 when I had no money at all
I borrowed it, loaned it and did anything I could, to stand tall

And stretch my mind and body to come up with solutions and a plan
there was no logical explanation for what I did, I ran. . .

With an idea, a deep sense of confidence that this was what I needed to do
I remembered that, on this morning, my mind flew

The seed had been planted deep
little by little I created ways to prep for the leap

Confidence is a ticket to happiness and motivation
without it, life loses its sensation

Confidence is belief in your dreams
it's more than the name seems

With confidence you take calculated risk
feel a skip in your step, a frisk

Metamorphosis Of A Misfit

Confidence makes you shiny and sunny
people think you're, charismatic and funny

Confidence can change your life in many ways
count the days

You've been confidently wearing your invisible cloak
the one providing you with a confidence soak

That seeps into your every pore
transporting you to more

To an über life of your dreams
where it seems like magical teams

Connect with you and stuff just happens
seemingly coincidentally, colluding with kins

Everything seems in perfect alignment
like it's been heaven sent

Not that this lasts forever and always
yet your resilience is strong with the passing days

Confidence is like a sensational safety net
allowing you to bounce back after a fall or discouraging bet

Confidence changes who you thought you were
puts you in touch with your inner whir

Metamorphosis Of A Misfit

The highest part of your being
it allows you to be all seeing

To shine light into the darkest of places
recognize and connect with inspirational faces

What will you accomplish with your new-found confidence cloak
will you be prosperous and proud or devastatingly broke

You have the power of choice
confidence gives heart, to your voice

Practice it and make it a habit
you'll be amazed and enthralled at the kit

You now posses for powers of your choosing
this is so much more than idle musing

With confidence, integrity and passion
you're capable and will experience satisfaction

On a higher level of a wondrous time line
wouldn't that experience be fine?

Conjure up your confidence
see what your competence. . .

draws to your energy and heart
take a stand, shine apart

Metamorphosis Of A Misfit

From others with no confidence at all
they'll be the ones that fall

Can't seem to pick themselves up
their thought is always half empty in their cup

There are always things out there, to bring you down
yet with your confidence capes on, you will not frown

Your spirits will soar
your motivation be so much more

Your confidence is key
to setting you free

Go get yours now, see what's in store
for you, your life and so much more

The effect you'll have on others will be two-fold
go follow your dreams - be bold

To review - confidence is key
just do it - you'll see!

Reflection Questions

1. Where do you experience tension and stress in your body? What let's you know, you're out of alignment?

   _____
   _____
   _____
   _____
   _____
   _____
   _____
   _____

2. What triggers or buttons do you have that cut you to the core?

   _____
   _____
   _____
   _____
   _____
   _____
   _____
   _____

3. When you feel you've been treated unfairly, how do you deal with it? How does your 'dealing with it' work out for you?

   _____
   _____
   _____
   _____
   _____

_____

_____

4. If you knew the answer to your problem, what would it be?

_____
_____
_____
_____
_____
_____
_____
_____

5. When you are draped in your 'confidence cape' what are you capable of?

_____
_____
_____
_____
_____
_____
_____
_____

6. If there's one thing you can tell your 5 year old self about confidence, what will it be?

_____
_____
_____
_____
_____
_____

7. How does your future look different when viewed from your confidence platform? What will you achieve?

___

Stress To Sublime

This is a continual pattern in my life! I tend to go 150% strong and then get; burned out, disheartened, depleted, and have a tendency to feel cheated. I'll come up with an amazing plan and work so hard to MAKE it work, when it doesn't I fall into a depth of despair and forget; who I am, what my purpose is, I feel flat, stressed, and negativity takes a stranglehold. I get so tangled in forcing, doing and fear that I forget about all the; joy, blessings, friends and family that love and support me. I feel trapped and ashamed, finding it difficult to reach out and ask for the support I crave. This poem was written when I caught myself in a stress cycle of despair and caught it before it sunk its teeth in! I remembered to remind myself that 'this too shall pass' and this place is not who I am, it's a part of my experience in the whole scheme of life. I remembered to recognize those phenomenal people in my life who are there for me, I just need to reach out. I remembered to look back and see how far I'd come. My sublime was closer than what I had feared, all I needed was a reminder that I have the power to make a choice and change the stress. Alchemizing stress to sublime may not happen all at once, yet when you practice persistence, amazing things will occur. Small consistent change WILL accumulate to have massive impact.

Metamorphosis Of A Misfit

Do you feel it
Being at the bottom of the pit

No matter what you do, you're stuck
frustration, making you want to scream F*#K

Ever wondered why you repeat the same patterns over and again
feel like your story of life, is written, with a tainted pen?

Stress can be sneaky, pervasive and severe
stress is so serious it can cause death to be near

We know too much stress affects our health
our productivity our vibrancy and our wealth

It's all around us like the elephant in the room
tension is thick, you're waiting for the - BOOM

Of everything exploding and falling apart
the sound of tearing, smashing and breaking of a heart

Stress can cause us to be snappy and curt
to disrespect those we love, causing pain and hurt

sometimes others around, have no idea of the stress we're under
we keep it buried, attempting to hide thunder!

How do you hide a powerful force, of rumbling magnitude
can you do this, without an abrupt, harsh attitude?

Metamorphosis Of A Misfit

Thunders powerful and loud
it'll be heard and is proud

What if you let your anger out
will you go crazy and insanely shout?

Will you explode and ruin your life?
will you feel like you're diving into undeniable strife?

will it feel grand to let it all go
will it be a relief, to not have to tow

The heavy burden of stress around
to be able to unhitch, feel released instead of bound

How will you let your stress out?
in a soundproof room, or with a resonating shout?

Will you smash things that weren't important to release tension
or take a class, relax into a deep meditation?

Are drugs the answer to numb your pain
to block out the world, dull your brain?

Will you be creative and write, paint or draw
which technique, do you give the highest score?

Maybe you want to hide and never some out
maybe you feel like sitting in a corner dreaming of a re-route

Metamorphosis Of A Misfit

Stress is dressed in many different wrappings
has a multitude of unique trappings

What will the effect of stress be on your life, in 5 years?
what about those around you - do they sense your fears?

Stress can be a killer and most unkind
it can also be rather incredible for your mind

Positive stress in the right dose for you
to motivate, inspire and allow you to do

What you may never have known you're capable of doing
the key is knowing, when to stop pursuing. . .

The kind of stress, eating away at your body, mind and soul
what's your biggest, tactical stress goal?

What will happen when your focus addresses stress
on relaxation solutions, and overhauling mess

What if NOT cutting ties was making you sick
imagine replacing them, with ones allowing you to pick. . .

And choose your direction in life
what if you released the strife?

How will it feel to be stress free
will you want to come fly with me?

Metamorphosis Of A Misfit

Take a trip through your life, take a peek at your future house
what'll you see, when stress is no longer an elephant, but a tiny mouse?

In 5 years time what do you see
will you be hiding or wanting to flee?

Will you be standing tall, proud and strong
singing from your heart, your own soulful song

In 5 years, who'll be at your side
choose your friends selectively and you'll experience an amazing ride

5 years ahead of now, how do you feel?
are you nourishing yourself with every meal?

Future pacing 5 years ahead
are you vibrant or closer to dead?

What's one message your future self would say
what can they share with you, to make your day?

Think about your future self 5 years from this time
not to do so, may be a crime!

To keep going, with your head in the sand
marching along with a soul-less band

Take time to reevaluate your choices and dreams
everything may not be as it seems

Metamorphosis Of A Misfit

Moving from stress to sublime
can change your life, it did mine!

There are; tools, techniques, steps, and a trick
to bring your life into alignment brick by brick

Feel into being sublime
keep that with you throughout time

Imagine into relaxation, peace and joy
your mind, much more powerful than a toy

Stress less and laugh often
before it's time to meet that coffin!

You want to be sure, you've lived a life worth living
that it's filled with purpose, love, compassion and giving

That you inspire those around you and live from the heart
that your days are meaningful and connected, not torn apart

You want to leave this world with a smile and a grin
knowing, your life was not a sin

This precious life, too succulent to waste
live with gratitude and a magnificent taste

Of pleasure infused magnanimous actions
combining skill sets, rather than walls of factions

Metamorphosis Of A Misfit

Be kind, smile
you don't know other people's mile

What they've encountered, experienced and felt
what matters is not the hand we were dealt

We have a choice to pick up and move onward
again and again, to use feedback to guide us and be rid

Of that, that does not serve our intentions well
release them, it's irrelevant how many times you fell

Brush it off, pick up and learn from your lesson taught
then you'll be free, not trapped or caught

From stress to sublime you'll go
how you do it, only you'll know

Take the time to experience release
see how it feels, to be at peace

I see in you, what you may not
there are times when maybe, you forgot

How incredibly talented you are
does that sound bizarre?

Do you feel uncomfortable with generous praise?
feel into it and amaze

Metamorphosis Of A Misfit

At your talents so fine
there's always someone thinking "I wish they were mine!"

Talk to your stress, acknowledge its presence
then release it and its essence

Know it's a guest who will visit again
until then

Hold close to your heart that you're divine, perfect and free
just like me

We're all connected on some level of universal bond
like ripples from a pristine pond

There's a chain reaction, with just one splash
imagine the effect and the generous cash

That occurs when we act from a place of sincerity
may your life be filled with serendipity

Go live, have fun, enjoy
this is not an empty ploy

You have the power to make your life brilliant
choose your color tint

Shine bright, brighter than ever before
that's the attraction, the law

Metamorphosis Of A Misfit

What you put out, comes back, simple physics
what will you put into your mix?

A dash of sunshine, pinch of authenticity
spoonful of courage and a cup of audacity?

From stress to sublime
I know you can climb

To the top of wherever it is, you want to be
go do it and a magnificent view you'll see

Climb with integrity and heart
that'll most certainly set you apart

As you look out from your view so clear
listen carefully and see what you hear

Is it nature, family, colleagues or friends
are there whispers of making amends?

Climb to your dreams and feel the sensation
of you being, on your favorite vacation

Soaking up the experience and feeling surrounded
by safety, love and being peacefully grounded

Sublime is yours in your deepest core
search and when found, open the door. . .

Metamorphosis Of A Misfit

To calm, energy abound
your life fully lived, is found

Surround yourself by those you adore
live happily ever after, for ever more

Reflection Questions

1. What will you feel when your stress is released?

   _____
   _____
   _____
   _____
   _____
   _____
   _____
   _____

2. What's stopping you from releasing your stress?

   _____
   _____
   _____
   _____
   _____
   _____
   _____
   _____

3. How is stress effecting your life and those around you?

   _____
   _____
   _____
   _____
   _____
   _____
   _____
   _____

4. What's the cost of NOT addressing your stress?

_____
_____
_____
_____
_____
_____
_____
_____

5. Who do you know that can assist you with stress reduction? How and when will you reach out to them?

_____
_____
_____
_____
_____
_____
_____
_____

6. What's your WHY for wanting to reduce stress?

_____
_____
_____
_____
_____
_____
_____
_____

7. What are you capable of, when your stress isn't ruling your life?

Piece of Peace

This is yet ANOTHER poem dealing with the organization that I had several negative experiences with! In hindsight, it's clear that it's not only what this company did, I was struggling within myself. I didn't have the confidence or belief in myself, to realize I was worth so much more than how this company treated me. I struggled with wanting the 'protection, recognition and safety net' of this well recognized organization, as well as knowing deep down, I needed and wanted to start my own company. As life often reveals over time, this experience was exactly what I needed, to push me into a direction I was too scared to take! It also provided lots of material for this book AND reminded me of all the tools, techniques and friends I have access to. It gave me a reminder that I get to choose and script my life, I could hang on and fight this injustice tooth and nail OR focus on what I really wanted, a thriving business of my own! I had the choice to stay mad and bitter OR to make choice after choice, to grow into a resilient person, and recalibrate my life, to one I love!

Metamorphosis Of A Misfit

I'm mad, hurt and hard done by
want to bury my head and cry

I want to let go
don't know which way to go

I want release, I want closure
I want what's mine, I'm losing my composure

I've gone through stages over the last few weeks
of feeling hatred, pain, valleys and peaks

Ups and downs are fine for a while
then they get draining, I lose my smile

My sparkle diminishes and fear sneaks in
I want to be free and rid of this sin

Sin as a category of the lowest form of who I know I am
robbing me of my essence, like a battering ram

It pounds away at my heart and soul
I know it would be beneficial to create a new goal

One with joy, love
from higher above

One with meaning and lightness
not in this lower state of mess

Metamorphosis Of A Misfit

I want a piece of peace in this torn up state
I want a piece of peace that is my fate

I know life's too precious, to hold onto anger and resentment
so here's my plan, it feels heaven sent

I've created a morning ritual of meditation, yoga and writing
this I know will help heal and stop the fighting

The torment in my head
it allows me to get out of bed

I smile knowing that it is a great way
to greet the morning each day

sometimes it's more forced than real
yet a routine it's become, that's the deal

The next step in my plan is vague
I want to forgive this plague

I want to release the pressure valve
of wanting, what I know, will never be a salve

For some things are not worth fighting for
they cause turmoil and start many a war

It's a fine line to know where to put that mark in the sand
I think I've found it, me and my merry band

Metamorphosis Of A Misfit

Of support crew, friends, family and networking pals
it's amazing how healing, the love from these gals

My husband's love
wraps around me like a glove

Knowing I'm surrounded by this angel pose
gives me the strength to not be so bossy

To release my anger, hurt and fear
into the wondrous atmosphere

I know karma will take its course
and I would rather be riding a horse

Or walking our dog
playing outside or photographing fog

A million things I can focus my intentions on
then soon this stress will be gone

I will take the higher ground
I have been lost and now found

Not in a church, in the love of my surroundings each day
in a uniquely incredible, universal way

There's a higher power, of that I'm sure
feeling into that love and support is my cure

Metamorphosis Of A Misfit

Knowing I don't have control over everything
believing that things are in perfect alignment makes my heart sing

Just quietly at first and a little shaken
yet I know I am not mistaken

In the strength of releasing with love to let life flow
embracing a piece of peace and letting the rest go

To hold onto the struggle would set me back
from my passion, joy and probably give me a heart attack

Or cause some such illness as stress often does
so I release with love and feel the buzz

Of harmony coming back into my being
and once again - I am clear seeing

I don't have the answers or all the clues
I do have some curious views

It's through this curiosity that the tension fades
loses its power and into the water it wades

Getting washed away and cleansed by the earth
allowing a kind of rebirth

Every day we can choose to be reborn
release our struggle and our scorn

Metamorphosis Of A Misfit

It may be a ceremony with your closest friends
it maybe private and that's how you make amends

However you choose to live a fresh new life
know that with a piece of peace you can release the knife

Put down the cutting edge
decide on a meaningful pledge

Get support and accountability
you may be amazed at your versatility

You're stronger and more loving than you can sometimes see
take a look around, ask your friends, set yourself free

Reflection Questions

1. When you feel an injustice in your life, what's your immediate reaction? What lets you know, you're experiencing inner turmoil?

   _____
   _____
   _____
   _____
   _____
   _____
   _____
   _____

2. What patterns do you notice with situations in your life, causing you stress or upset?

   _____
   _____
   _____
   _____
   _____
   _____
   _____
   _____

3. When everything seems upside down, stressful and sad, what tools or techniques do you have access to?

   _____
   _____
   _____
   _____
   _____
   _____

4. Although you may intellectually KNOW, how to move from a place of stress and stuck-ness, this doesn't mean you do it! What advice would you give someone when they're feeling out of sorts?

5. If you think of yourself 5 years from now, what do you see? Where are you and what are you doing? What feeling do you get from the future you? What's ONE thing, the future you will tell the present you, about how to get to where you want to be?

6. If you were to focus on what you want, where you want to be, how you want to feel, what will this look like? If you're writing a brief character description of YOU in a book, what would you like people to know about phenomenal YOU? Remember it's YOUR story, you get to mould and create your character into whatever you want!

_____
_____
_____
_____
_____
_____
_____
_____
_____

7. What's the COST to you, of staying right where you are? What's the cost to your friends and family, of you staying right where you are now? Who in your life will be most affected when you make a change and embody the person you were born to be?

_____
_____
_____
_____
_____
_____
_____
_____
_____
_____
_____
_____

-Magnanimous Love-

Joy Of Zen

Jason Kotecki asked me a question one day when I was visiting his wife and adorable kids. He asked "What were you most surprised about when you became a parent?" This questions flawed me, as I didn't know how to answer it. I'd been a nanny for years in my 20's, so had experience with the raising of tiny humans. I gave some answer and everyday after my visit, I kept asking myself Jason's question - like I was on a quest to find an answer I felt satisfied with! One day it happened, finally I realized and remembered the most surprising thing about being a parent. This thing I had not anticipated or even imagined it's power. The most surprising thing for me, is the JOY our daughter Zennia brings to the world. I say world as I post photos and videos on Face Book, so my friends and family overseas can feel more connected with her. This poem is about the joy of Zen!

Metamorphosis Of A Misfit

From the moment you entered this world and we held you tight
you were the most enchanting sight

Your tiny fingers and sweet toes
only an angel knows

How it came to be
that you are such a sweet pea

As you grew and your smile appeared
it melted hearts from everyone loving and feared

You made homeless men smile with glee
as you smiled at them happily

You made grumpy people turn
their snarls into softness and learn

That they too can be touched by such an old soul
with wisdom deep, there's no control

Over the magical power you exuded
you ensured everyone was included

You bridged gaps of age
calmed rage

Gave people pause to reflect on the beauty of life
allowed those with deep strife

Metamorphosis Of A Misfit

To look upon you and say 'This is a reflection of everything good'
I had no idea, you would. . .

Touch the hearts of so many
sweet little angel Zennie

We love you so much and you are such a gift
I'm sure you can heal any rift

With just your presence and calm
your smile like a soothing balm

We love you so much and are amazed every day
at what you do and say

You bring joy to our neighbors as we walk around
your laugh is an intoxicating sound

I've taken you to networking events since you were a few weeks young
your praises were so highly sung

That if I ever went without you
people were kind of true. . .

In saying that it was nice to see me
and, where's your sweet baby?

We want to watch her grace
she's such an addition to the human race

Metamorphosis Of A Misfit

I swear, I'm not making this up, what a wild ride!
your joy, little fish is spread far and wide

You melt hearts and people are amazed at your feats
your snowboarding and skateboarding, such treats

For people to marvel over and say
'we're going to see her at the Olympics one day!'

The joy you bring the world sweet Zen
is more stars than ten out of ten

It's off the charts ridiculous, how good looking you are
you are an inspirational star

From recycled stardust we're all created
yet we weren't all rated

The same
you're to blame

For others wondering how you embody so much joy
when all you do is play with a toy!

You're our sweet baby loves that we adore
and people want to see you more and more!

The world is brighter with you in it
and for that I think of you and pivot

Metamorphosis Of A Misfit

In happiness for you being our daughter
life without you is not even a quarter

As much fun
as seeing you run

Jump, play
doing things your way

Looking at me with your Daddy's sparkling blue eyes
it's no surprise

To me
that you bring so much glee

I just hadn't factored in the effect you'd have on a stranger
you sense no danger

I think that's one thing that's unique about you
you feel and do. . .

You high five strangers and make their day
it's your sweet baby way

To make wondrous connections
and share affections

So Mr Kotecki, I finally have an answer for you
I truly do!

Metamorphosis Of A Misfit

The joy our little Zen can bring
makes my heart sing

Her power
to admire a flower

To take life and run with it
her zest and heart lit

With passion, love and a depth of life
unfathomable and rife

Your mannerisms infectious and delightful
I cannot wait till

You spread joy throughout the land
and with a healing hand

Bridge the gap between war and peace
may you cease

All hurtful views
dancing in your tutus

No pressure, I see you doing this with ease
you know I only tease

For the joy you bring sweet Zen
is straight from heaven

Reflection Questions

1. Who and what brings joy to you?

   _____
   _____
   _____
   _____
   _____
   _____
   _____

2. How do you define joy?

   _____
   _____
   _____
   _____
   _____
   _____
   _____

3. What happens when you encounter joy unexpectedly in your day?

   _____
   _____
   _____
   _____
   _____
   _____
   _____

4. How do you bring joy to the world, your community or your family?

   _____
   _____
   _____
   _____
   _____
   _____
   _____
   _____

5. What do you notice when you bring someone joy?

   _____
   _____
   _____
   _____
   _____
   _____
   _____
   _____

6. What is life like devoid of joy?

   _____
   _____
   _____
   _____
   _____
   _____
   _____
   _____

7. What can you do this week or next to spread joy in a delightful way? Spend 5 minutes Googalizing 'how to spread Joy', it's phenomenal and heartwarming!

_____
_____
_____
_____
_____
_____
_____
_____
_____
_____
_____
_____
_____
_____
_____
_____
_____
_____
_____
_____
_____
_____
_____
_____
_____

Love of My Life

This poem is inspired by my incredible husband Cris Blattner! It's easy to take phenomenal people in your life for granted. To lean on them and get swept away with life and all that it entails. The circumstances of how we met, were reconnected and the barriers we faced in being together, ALMOST make it impossible to not be grateful every day, for all that we have. In saying this, I know I DO take this incredible man for granted at times. I choose to make our relationship as strong, sexy and sensational as it can possibly be! Simple to do, yes, easy, not so much! Between; work, running a business, house chores, a beautiful daughter, friends, family, pets and LIFE, sometimes love gets lost along the way. The good news is that it is never far away and can be found and rediscovered, over and over again! The key to keeping relationships a priority in life's chaos - remembering to remind each other, we have a KEY! It's easy to forget how important it is to celebrate, communicate and KISS. When you remember you have a magical key to unlock the love you share together, you'll be blessed and amazed at creative ways to love each other in the most trying of times!

Metamorphosis Of A Misfit

What other powerful force
can change your directional course

What higher power is there
if not love everywhere

Can you imagine if all wars were love celebrations
if all armies were love facilitators throughout the nations

Love is a healing energy field
that can make the strongest of us yield

Love makes us rethink our innermost core value
rationalize that which may be polar to what we preciously believed, let me tell you

Things people do for love is immense
there's not a strong or high enough fence

To keep love out
it makes people cheer and shout

There's no ordinary love anywhere
travel the world and you will hear

Amazingly heartfelt stories that will melt the toughest old heart
love is wisdom, healing, and sets us apart

Let me tell you my story of the love of my life
Cris is now my husband and me his wife

Metamorphosis Of A Misfit

We met at Chippewa Ranch Camp in Rhinelander
I lived in Australia and thought I would take a gander!

Check this US of A out
see what it's all about

In 1996 I flew from Perth to LA, LA to Chicago
I arrived at camp and thought, so. . .

This is the North Woods, I love it
I can stay here with my pack and kit

The camp had such an impact, I went back in 2001
thought I'd experience more crazy fun!

I had no idea what I was in for and it would forever change me
my little campers went home and Porter Camp rolled in with glee

My heart skipped a beat and my senses aroused, what was the fuss?
the most incredible being I'd ever seen, stepped off the bus!

His eyes of the brightest blue
is golden skin glowed, my heart flew

I couldn't explain my immediate reaction, I felt pinned
it was love at first sight, or so I imagined

I'd never experienced anything quite like it, heaven I was seeing!
I wasn't alone in my admiration of this amazing being

Metamorphosis Of A Misfit

I quickly learned that every girl with a pulse thought he was the best
I also found out, he did not have a girlfriend, this was a test

I was an introvert at heart
and not sure how to set myself apart

It happened on dance night, this little 8-year-old girl with long red hair
looked at Cris with a glazed over stare

She asked him if he would dance with her, he said yes
he made her feel like a princess

That was it, I was officially in love
it felt like a sign from the heavens above

Porter camp was only two weeks, so we soon parted ways
my head and heart ached, I was in a daze

Through teary eyes, I said good bye staring at the floor
he said, "does it have to be forever more?"

We arranged to meet up, after camp pack up was done
the next week was full of immense love, travel and fun

We went to a wedding on Lake Superior
someone told us, we looked more in love than the married pair!

I was like a creepy stalker watching him as he slept
tears trickled down my face as I knew there was no time left

Metamorphosis Of A Misfit

My visa was running out and I had to move on
next stop was Washington DC, with my friend Carrie Donovan

We'd meet at summer camp in 96
I hadn't seen her since that summer camp fix

As I was out sightseeing, looking at the Pentagon
a crazy surreal nightmare went on

September 11th occurred
it seems so absurd

I thought I would die, that world war 3 would occur, causing pain
the love of my life, I'd never see again

Phone lines were jammed and it took some time
to realize, I'd be just fine

I sent Cris an e mail saying I wanted to come back to him
life was too short and I'd experienced grim

Unfortunately he didn't get my e mail in time, to Switzerland I flew
my best friend lived there and work I needed to pursue

My life was shattered and Cris and I grew apart
fast forward to 2009, I wasn't so smart

I managed to get myself into an awful mess
financially, relationship wise and take a guess

Metamorphosis Of A Misfit

I was still in love with the memory of Cris
no one could compare and I would dream of his kiss

The unthinkable happened my Swiss friend Kat
passed away, just like that

Actually, it'd been years with Hodgkinson's Disease
she was only in her thirties

I went into shock, anger, sadness then depression, my body shook
through a crazy series of events, I found out Kat died on Face Book

I wanted to let all our mutual friends know, so they didn't find out the same way
I made phone calls, wrote e mails and letters, then came the day. . .

I thought of Cris, my summer camp love of 10 years ago
I felt I needed to tell him of Kat's passing, so. . .

I e-mailed him to give him the news
he wrote a few lines that rocked my small world views

I had no idea of his life situation or him of mine
I think it took a few weeks of e mails before I asked him to dine

With me for dinner, it seemed irrelevant that I was in Oz, him in the USA
I just wanted to be with him and hear him say

Anything in that American lilt
he spoke with a warm embrace, like in a comforting quilt

Metamorphosis Of A Misfit

So in 2010 I flew to the States
although 10 years apart, we were still best of mates

We took up from where we left off, I missed my buddy
in 2011 I moved here to study

We were married in 2013 on Lake Superior, happier I could not be
death drew us together and love saved me

Every day, I appreciate our love, friendship, joy and laughter
it took a long time and was worth the wait for my perfect partner

I feel we have a unique relationship
I would not be where I am today without this trip

This journey of a lifetime, love is strange
it provides a full range

Of emotions, strengths, weaknesses and pride
what an incredibly amazing ride

Love for me is; support, respect, affection, empowerment and joy
there couldn't be a happier girl and boy

Husband and wife means so much more
than a piece of legal paper and I swore

That I'd remember this always and be grateful for the love of my life
though there's been joy, also strife

Metamorphosis Of A Misfit

I'm forever grateful of life, love and my amazing husband Cris
always and forever I remember our first kiss

He's assisted me through moving to another country
getting legal alien residency

The joys and heartbreaks that come with being a solo-preneur
he is such a divine lure

No matter how sad, angry or broken I feel
he always offers me a better deal

Gives me some insight
to see the light

In a dark situation of which I felt blind
he is made from pure kind

Did I mention he studied aeronautic engineering?
as if he could get any more endearing

My Mum thinks the sun shines out of his rear
I have to agree on this topic - it's clear

That the man is a super human and I the luckiest being
maybe love is all seeing

We have our faults, some more than others
that doesn't mean we can't be the best of lovers

Metamorphosis Of A Misfit

Love to me, is freedom and kind
it's meaningful in soul, body and mind

I feel blessed to have found the love of my life
and am indeed the happiest wife!

Love lifts me up, supports me and treats me fine and well
and that's all I have to tell!

Reflection Questions

1. What's love for you?
   _____
   _____
   _____
   _____
   _____
   _____
   _____
   _____

2. What allows you to feel loved? How do you know when someone loves you?
   _____
   _____
   _____
   _____
   _____
   _____
   _____
   _____

3. When you are in love, how do you resolve conflicts? How is this different when you feel OUT of love?
   _____
   _____
   _____
   _____
   _____
   _____

4. What defense mechanisms do you have, when it comes to love? What areas would you LOVE to change?

_____
_____
_____
_____
_____
_____
_____
_____

5. What's the most loving; act, gesture, words or adventure, someone has given/shown you?

_____
_____
_____
_____
_____
_____
_____

6. Who's a person you trust completely when you are feeling; stressed, depressed, anxious, or scared? This person is someone who won't judge you and will give you advice to heal your soul.

_____
_____
_____
_____

7. When you're feeling brave and vulnerable, what things would you like to share with the love of your life?

Zen Fish

This poem is self explanatory and inspired by our daughter Zennia. I'm not sure why we call her a fish, it's something we've done since her birth. She is a sweet angel and I want to be very conscious of not letting my emotions and problems flow onto her as if she is the cause of my stress. On so many levels she is the most amazing blessing we could have ever hoped and dreamed of. She's strong, inspiring and a magnificent teacher. She's two as I edit this and I'm sure I've learned way more from her than I could ever teach her. I know my actions speak louder than words and I pray I can act in a way that is a role model suitable for such an awesome being.

Metamorphosis Of A Misfit

Oh little Zen fish you come from the sea
you my love are a spirit free

I gaze into your eyes like the ocean
get lost and close to frozen

For the depth and intrigue is mesmerizing
your soul tantalizing

I wonder what thoughts it is that you think
I wonder as you thirstily drink

I sometimes see a glimpse of your future fate
you are strong, bright and have a full plate

Will you juggle life in a way that is satisfying?
Will you be happy trying?

I have no way to know
and yet I feel it deep below

The surface of my skin
I feel akin

To you Baby Girl Blattner
I wish for you the world and a happy ever after

I catch myself dreaming of you when you're older
of our relationship and even bolder

Metamorphosis Of A Misfit

I dream of who you will be
I wonder if you will flee

As I did in my life
I hope you don't follow my strife

I hope your clear sparkling eyes, see more than I do
your dreams realized, I wish this for you

I wonder how much impact I have on your being
what are your sweet eyes seeing?

You're 6 and a half months young
do you remember, words from my tongue?

Do you feel the tears that drip from my face to yours?
you are not the cause

Most of all I don't want this to reflect on you
my deep ocean love, it's true

I love you more deeply than life can see
my tears are my struggles within me

I worry I will not be a role model for you
I fear I won't have a clue

I struggle with the balance of being a Mummy
and providing for all to have a full tummy

Metamorphosis Of A Misfit

Lucky for us we're provided for
we are not rich & we are not poor

I worry I can't provide enough too
I worry I'll be unsatisfied and blue

It's not your fault for causing my conflict
this was here before you pict

Your time to enter this universe
these problems, my curse

It's mine alone
you warm my heart when I see how you've grown

Just over 6 months and you are so strong
you are determined and can do no wrong

In my eyes you are a perfect being
a radiant glow of all seeing

An energy of bliss
and with a kiss

A day can turn from cloudy grey to sparkling blue
this is such a gift I love from you

When I'm networking or away for a while
I come back to your smile

Metamorphosis Of A Misfit

It warms my heart like no other
I know you're an angel under cover

Everyone you meet falls in love with you Zen
you are a perfect 10!

This is not to say
you are always this way

We all have our moments of bliss and sad
although it makes me sparkle to see you and your Dad

He's so proud of you and loves you more than you may know
I tell you this now as then when you grow

You'll know how much you were loved right from the start
a love like a bulls eye to a spectacular dart

You have changed our lives - that's for sure
you tiny Zen are so pure

You see little things in life and smile with glee
your heart is infinite and free

I want you to know that I'll do my best
to pass the motherhood test

I set the bar high
and I know why

Metamorphosis Of A Misfit

I want to give you the gift of passion
I never want you to feel lack and ration

I want you to shine bright
to live large and not in fright

I want you to choose your most passionate path
to always get pleasure from the bubbles in your bath

To reach for the stars
and feel safe shooting for Mars

I want you to embrace your unique essence and power
to blossom like the exquisite flower

That you are
I love you even when we're far

You are etched into my every fibre
and in an instant I am transformed to a tiger

Who will protect you always and forever
little Zen Fish you are so clever

You choose your destiny
you choose to sparkle effervescently

I love you so much it hurts inside
I know this life will be a wonderful ride

Metamorphosis Of A Misfit

There will be ups with the downs
there will be smiles with the frowns

That's ok for you and me
the bright side we will see

I look forward to growing with you
and seeing where our North true

Takes us in this odyssey
be who you want to be

I'll do the same
maybe I can tame

My wild Gremlin brain
and move into the cruise lane

Where I can stop being so frantic
chillax and be less pedantic

See you there my baby Zen Fish
for you are, my dream and wish

Reflection Questions

1. What's your favorite childhood memory?

   _____
   _____
   _____
   _____
   _____
   _____
   _____

2. What's some advice (or comfort) you wish someone had given you when you were 5 years old?

   _____
   _____
   _____
   _____
   _____
   _____
   _____

3. What's an area of your life that you feel a great deal of pressure to not fu*% it up?

   _____
   _____
   _____
   _____
   _____
   _____
   _____

4. Do you have memories of your childhood that you wish were different? How would that change who you are now?

_____
_____
_____
_____
_____
_____
_____

5. If you grew up in a 'perfect environment' for you to thrive, what different choices would you have made in life?

_____
_____
_____
_____
_____
_____
_____

6. When you see through the eyes of a child or pet you love deeply, how does that make the world a different place?

_____
_____
_____
_____
_____
_____

7. If you were to forgive someone from your childhood, who would it be and why? Remember that by not forgiving, you're 'poisoning' yourself. To forgive is NOT forgetting or condoning what was done, more of a release and recognition that the person did the best they could with their mental health, education and life experience. It may never justify their behavior, it's looking toward your future and lightening your baggage to maximize your odyssey!

-Future Footprints-

Scripting Your Story

This poem was inspired by going to MOTH story telling events. I love the idea of these and if you've not heard of them, googalize it! At the end of the story's, some one will say "Hope you have a story worthy week." I love this! It reminds me, we all have the choice to create a life we love. Despite our situations, there are always ways to recalibrate our state. I love to remind myself of this when I feel stuck! There's so much power in knowing you have choice. It doesn't need to be a massive life shift, it can literally be 5 minutes done consistently. Small changes done consistently can have massive impacts. How will you live a story worthy life?

Metamorphosis Of A Misfit

What characteristics to you see
when creating your personality?

How will you describe yourself to a stranger?
corporate type, entrepreneur or maybe a ranger

When you imagine deeply and with play
what do you see that makes your day?

What location are you located?
to what are you devoted?

Is this life similar to the one you live now?
tell me how

Is it worlds apart from where you are today?
if I may

What stops you from living your story book life?
does it cause strife?

To live a life half lived, kind of strange
what will happen if you take steps to change?

What needs to be in place
in order for you to escape the rat race?

Take a moment to imagine the ideal you
what will you do

Metamorphosis Of A Misfit

If you become
the person you aspire to be and then some?

If you can dream it, write it and feel it inside
why not take the adventurous ride?

Throw caution to the wind and feel free
what will it be

That will allow you to feel you've made it in life
diminishing your strife

Allowing an openness for new opportunity
a chance to recalibrate and find a community

That fills your soul and allows you to energize
is it moving or maybe a downsize?

Whatever it may be
this is what I see

You taking steps to creating a life worth living
a dream life where you can be giving

Of your time, finances, love or whatever you choose
what have you got to lose?

Some of us forget we have the power
to script our life in less than an hour!

Metamorphosis Of A Misfit

Well at least make a start
that's what sets you apart

From the majority of crew
who unlike you

Don't take any time to create themselves at all
they lose sight of the big and focus on the small

They forget their dream, passion and ideal
they settle, compromise and feel

Life passing them by for a variety of reasons
the change of seasons

Sometimes gives them pause
to remember a cause

That was once dear to their hearts
the focus on excuses rather than parts

Parts that are changeable
shiftable and malleable

Sections of life that it's possible to take a different view
to see anew

Things that once seemed permanent and fixed
now are pliable and can be mixed

Metamorphosis Of A Misfit

With a fresh mindset and reframe
you can retrain your game

So as you imagine a story of your life being created
think of the traits you want to have associated

To who and what you are
what you stand for and what takes you far

What character to you play
in your everyday?

If there's one thing you would change TODAY, what will it be?
take the opportunity

To see a brand new perspective
shift your objective

Allow the unimaginable to come out and play
what do you say?

Ready to sculpt, carve, recalibrate and take a chance?
is it time to break your trance?

Of a life with clipped wings
you have the power to choose things

Things that are meaningful to you
what will you do

Metamorphosis Of A Misfit

With your choice?
is it purchasing a horse or Rolls Royce?

Is it carving out family time
to live a life more sublime?

What's your price of admission?
your latest edition

Of compromise made in good intention
yet you feel it like an ugly extension

Knowing it's not what you truly want or need
yes indeed

Life passes by at a certain pace
do you want it to be a race?

Do you want to take time to be present
to enjoy life and represent

Or keep going as you are
knowing inside that you wont get far?

Remember to remind yourself, you have a choice
you can be miserable or rejoice

This doesn't need to be, in a rose colored glasses way
unless that would add awesome, to your day?

Metamorphosis Of A Misfit

It's more about not staying stuck
having tools and techniques to wade through the muck

Having resources and time
to create a rhyme

Or whatever allows you to shine bright
some might say, they're right

They can't or it's too hard and they'd be correct
look at what thoughts you inject

Into your being
it may be freeing

To say anythings possible
where thoughts are transposable

It's your book, your life, you do as you please
you have the powerful keys

To create a most magnificent view
the most phenomenal you

So script wisely and with joy
like life is a toy!

You're the creator and author of your journey
not an attorney

Metamorphosis Of A Misfit

Or other well meaning being
YOU choose, what you'll be seeing

If you choose one way and it doesn't work out
make a U turn and scout

Write in pencil so erases can be made
rip off that band-aid!

Create a character that you're proud to be
create a life that like a tree

In time will grow strong and provide many gifts
create less rifts

Be a character that forgives
and outlives

The limiting beliefs of your past
start now, go fast

Why wait?
you may already be late!

There's always time, no matter your predicament
be vigilant

Take charge
live large!

Metamorphosis Of A Misfit

Reflection Questions

1. Write a description of an ideal you, fill it with as many details as possible?

   _____
   _____
   _____
   _____
   _____
   _____
   _____
   _____
   _____
   _____
   _____
   _____

2. What's your 'characters mission in life?

   _____
   _____
   _____
   _____
   _____
   _____

3. If someone's reading the book of you, what do you want them to take away from your story? How do you want them to feel about your 'character?'

4. Where does you story take place? Remember to let your imagination run totally wild, release the need to be practical in any sense!

5. If you were to take one section of your ideal story book of your life and turn it into an actual reality, what place will you start?

6. What's one tiny step you can take NOW, to make your life closer to it's ideal?

_____
_____
_____
_____
_____
_____

7. In your ideal story book life, what's the most fun section for you to focus on? Is it the setting, your career, family, finances, adventures or another area? Write details about this.

_____
_____
_____
_____
_____
_____
_____
_____
_____
_____
_____
_____
_____
_____
_____
_____
_____

Future You

One of my favorite activities to do when speaking and training, is called Future Pacing. This is an NLP (neuro-linguistic programming) technique that's incredibly powerful. It's taping into your subconscious and allowing you to visualize the future you. It's in alignment with what sports psychologists use allowing people to optimize their performance. The neat thing about this activity is that each time you do it, you may have different results! This poem is a journey of my own future pacing.

Metamorphosis Of A Misfit

I'm walking down a sandy path
with worn wooden railings, I hear a faint laugh

In the distance, it's drawing me near
the suns shining, my feet warm, in the grainy sand, the water crystal clear

I arrive at a T junction with ocean stretched as far as I can see
I chose to go left and allow my feet to take me

Along the shoreline of tepid water
I'm reminded of my beautiful daughter

I get back on track and look left to the grey worn verandah
I take a mental memoranda

I want to remember this feeling and place
the rustic, magnificent space

I'm about to reach my future self in 5 years time
I feel excitement and an aura of sublime

I walk up the wide, smooth wooden step
there she is, softly resounding respect

In a light, flowing white cotton summer dress
she stands tall looking noblesse

Her skin sun kissed, her hair wavy and long
her bare arms lean and strong

Metamorphosis Of A Misfit

Her feet bare
her persona, without a care

She seems light, happy, serene and grounded
she's surrounded

By minimalism, love and light
her green eyes shimmering bright

I ask her to share one thing with me
vital information to set me free

What's one thing that allowed her to get where she is
what's the answer to this quiz?

The answer that'll allow me to get to where you are
the answer that'll take me far

I listened closely to her words of wisdom
knowing they're my key to hacking the system

She laughed with heart and said this to me
"this is what will set you free"

Follow your heart and intuition
this will lead, to your fruition

Take a stand even when others are sitting
it's your uniqueness that'll stop the bullshitting

Metamorphosis Of A Misfit

The frustration you feel to mould yourself into who you're not
you'll find your place being perfectly you, your sweet spot

Trust this will happen and anchor your serenity
to access it later when it's necessary

To believe and to pick yourself up after a fall
stay strong, I know it's been a long haul

Follow those who you admire most
soon you'll be able to coast

In the knowing that your struggles are solved
your problems resolved

Peace is close by, stand your ground
your dreams'll be discovered and found

You have a gift
treasure it and sift

Through opportunities, not in alignment
with your life assignment

Smile more, relax and create white space
shift your pace

She placed her hands on my shoulders and looked deep in my soul
she said three words, "trust your role"

Metamorphosis Of A Misfit

We hugged and with a tear of gratitude
I said good bye and felt renewed

My spirit felt childlike and at peace, yet driven
as I went to leave, a gift I was given

I took the white washed paper wrapped present
with the ocean blue velvet ribbon with stamp of a pheasant

I thanked the future me
profusely

Stepped down the smooth wooden step toward the beach
I finally felt my dream future was within reach

I feel a sense of intense calm and peace
a massive release

My smile was ridiculously wide
as I strolled in the ankle deep tide

I turned right to go down the track with the smooth wood rails
returning to the original trails

That would guide me back to the here and now
I stopped next to a wooden bench seat and took a vow

To remember this tranquil feeling and succumb
anchor the moment with my finger and thumb

Metamorphosis Of A Misfit

As unravelling the gift
my mind was adrift

The magical sparkles sprinkled on my thighs
tears of happiness filled my eyes

My gift was a reflection of my future self and dreams
all is most certainly not as it seems

As I packed up my perfect treasure
journeying down the sandy path at my leisure

I knew that everything would be ok
my fears were placed at bay

I reached my present state and pushed open the gate
with my eyes now open I knew I could satiate

My highest wishes, hopes and dreams
to create sensational teams

To assist in building a magnificent legacy
filled with teachings and awesome chemistry

I love the fact, I can return to my future self, at any time
record my experience with a rhyme

What will your future self, 5 years from now, reveal to you?
how will this change what you believe to be true?

Metamorphosis Of A Misfit

Reflection Questions

1. Describe yourself 5 years from now?

   _____
   _____
   _____
   _____
   _____
   _____
   _____
   _____
   _____
   _____
   _____
   _____
   _____

2. What location is the future you in? What do your surroundings look like?

   _____
   _____
   _____
   _____
   _____
   _____
   _____
   _____

3. If there's one piece of advice your future self shares with you what'll it be?

   _____
   _____

4. If your future self gave you a gift that allowed insight into your future, what is it?

5. If there's a limited belief, stopping you from living your best life possible, what's one way to reframe it?

6. What's one thing your future self can tell you that'll make you smile and look forward to the future?

_____
_____
_____
_____
_____

7. What are steps you'll take, to allow you to get to the place of your future self? These may be minute or massive! When will you activate these steps?

_____
_____
_____
_____
_____
_____
_____
_____
_____
_____
_____
_____
_____
_____

Stop It

When my friend Carrie and I were going through our coaching training, we watched a video making fun of coaches/therapists and clients (https://www.youtube.com/watch?v=MDpyS2HN5SA) It was a coach who basically told his client to "STOP IT" every time she tried to tell him something! This made us laugh, not only at the video, at ourselves for being so absurd at times. We still use this affectionately on each other when we are stuck and getting in our own way! It's not always as simple as 'stopping it,' yet a humorous reminder, how simple some solutions can be.

Metamorphosis Of A Misfit

Stop it!
stop it

Oh you didn't hear me, let me say it again
let me get a pen. . .

I'll write it down for you
STOP IT when you're feeling blue

Stop it, when you're self hating
stop it when you're rating. . .

Yourself on a scale
wanting to bail. . .

From what matters most to you
I've been there too

I'm not saying don't feel your feelings and honor their place
I'm saying don't let them win the race

Stop it when you're being mean to you
you don't know what to do

Stop the blame and stop the shame
it's ok to be the same. . .

As when you were a small child
don't get riled. . .

Metamorphosis Of A Misfit

By your ego mind
stop getting caught up and find. . .

What's most important in your odyssey
stop getting stuck and wanting to flee

Stay with the trail
until you nail. . .

Your dreams till they come true
you owe this to you

Stop getting lost in self pity
stop being witty. . .

When you're dying inside
show some pride

Live large and tall
not just for you, for all. . .

That have gone before you and blazed a track
your tribe has your back. . .

Whether you know it or not
you've got to stop. . .

Staying stuck and stagnant
blaming life for your lack of flint

Metamorphosis Of A Misfit

Your spark your gift to this universe
there is a limitless purse. . .

You have access to with time, belief, effort and support
don't give up on your gifts that you fought. . .

So hard to make come to fruition
stop your self deprecating sin

Stop telling yourself you can't when you can
you can do anything you plan

Anything you dream
find tribe to be on your team

You're amazing, beautiful and unique
when you speak

You have wisdom to share
you care

So stop feeling stuck and sad
get mad. . .

If that's what you need to do
to motivate you

Get out there and live larger than life
cause some strife

Metamorphosis Of A Misfit

Make a difference and rock your view
it's ultimately you. . .

That will change the world, one person at a time
you will be sublime

Stop waiting for everything to be in line
a perfect sign

So do what Nike does and just do it
what's your bit. . .

To add to this journey we call life
stop it with the knife. . .

The cutting inflictions
love your inner convictions

You've got this, I know you do
go make a difference as too few. . .

Stay the path and go the distance
stop with the excuses, get a glimpse

Of the spectacular future you
that's right, the one that CAN do. . .

Whatever it is that lights your fire
surges your desire

Metamorphosis Of A Misfit

Makes you sing with glee
all I can do is plea

You stay with your passion
make it happen

It may be different from how you first thought
that doesn't mean you haven't caught. . .

The right idea at the right time
don't stop your climb

Keep it going and when you want to stop
stop it! Rise to the top

You got this
I send you bliss

For your journey whatever it may be
you see. . .

This life needs more passion and authenticity
give all your audacity

Then you'll know you are free
that's the best, you can be

Giving others the gift of your presence
your essence

Metamorphosis Of A Misfit

Stop with the giving up
be first rate and fill your cup

From your overflow
others will grow

Be you and do it to the best you can
take a stand and a plan

You've got this when you give it your all
stand tall. . .

Dream big then multiply it by one hundred
that's what all the greats did

You've got it in you I know
just go. . .

Be your best
stop the test

Shine bright
take flight

Who will benefit most from you soaring high
stop with the wanting to cry

I'm all for tears and not when they're debilitating
if you need some recalibrating. . .

Metamorphosis Of A Misfit

Get that done
shine like the sun

Soar like an eagle high
be like Yoda - forget TRY

Stop with the limits and cannot's
you're a phenomenal being

Don't deny others your gifts so rare
stop living small and pretending you don't care

About living life large and grand
lending a helping hand

To the area you are most drawn to
I believe in you

Reflection Questions

1. If there was one thing you would like to stop doing or believing, what would it be?

   _____
   _____
   _____
   _____
   _____
   _____
   _____

2. If you stopped believing something you told yourself repetitively, how will that change your life?

   _____
   _____
   _____
   _____
   _____
   _____
   _____

3. Who in your life will benefit most from you recalibrating your limited beliefs?

   _____
   _____
   _____
   _____
   _____
   _____
   _____

4. When you're in a state of mind, that you're capable and ready to unleash your super powers into this world, what'll be the first thing you do?

_____
_____
_____
_____
_____
_____
_____
_____

5. If you stopped listening and putting energy into your Gremlin Brain's beliefs, what new beliefs would there be room for?

_____
_____
_____
_____
_____
_____
_____
_____

6. How will you change your self talk, to be as compassionate as speaking to a young child you love?

_____
_____
_____
_____
_____

7. When you visualize your self 5 years from now, knowing you are practicing compassionate self talk, how do you see yourself? What are you doing and who are you assisting? Where are you and how are you feeling?

_____

-Visualizations-

Childlike Lens

This poem was inspired by a book I read by SARK (I love all her books) and she recommended carrying a photo of a little you. This is done as a reminder to speak to yourself nicely, as if you were speaking to that sweet little you! I loved this concept and dug out a 'special' little me in a 70's brown floral dress and white sandals. The sun is in my eyes and I'm squinting. I can feel the vulnerability in this photo, I see the naivety and the sweet innocence of someone who's three. Our daughter is 19 months, I remind myself to speak in the same encouraging, respectful, loving way, when I self talk. This is not normal for me and takes constant practice to not rip myself to shreds! Tiny baby steps, I love practicing and playing with being childlike, it's a stress reliever and technique to not take life and myself so seriously!

Metamorphosis Of A Misfit

What if one day you woke
and when you spoke

Your voice was that of you, when you were young
your mouth only spoke from a little ones tongue

Your eyes saw everything as mystical and fun
bubbles and magic and energy to run

All your problems were still there
and you would just stare

Like mesmerized in a daydream
so fanciful and free, your friends on your team

Knowing one day you will be
awesome and free

The most amazing version of you
there is no doubt this is true

When you look out the window, you see an array of hues
anything and everything is possible, you see the clues

To follow a path that's fun and adventure filled
your days a plethora of castles to build

Your childlike vision sees; rainbows, unicorns, and mermaids
shooting stars and magical trades

Metamorphosis Of A Misfit

You don't see troubles, you see solutions and songs
there are no wrongs. . .

Only lessons learned and smiles bright
what an incredible sight. . .

To see through a childlike lens
to jump in puddles and make amends

Without over analyzing and going crazy
seeing things in beautiful shades of hazy

Laying in freshly cut grass on a blanket so smooth
smiling at the sun and feeling your groove

Hugging pets and people as you see fit
doing your bit. . .

To bring so much joy to people you meet
that's no easy feat

Yet when you're little, you do this with ease
you play, joke and tease

What if you took time to see through a childlike lens, some day
what problems will you solve and will you run away?

To a place where dreams seem possible
be fantastically suasible

Metamorphosis Of A Misfit

When you're in this place of a tiny human being
what will you feel, what are you seeing?

Looking through different eyes
my be a brilliant surprise

You may find solutions where problems lay
smiles that last all day

Fabulous outfits that are frivolous and fun
a life where you don't need a gun

To protect yourself or your family
a magical place that sets you free

What if you just spend a minute
going back to a time when you saw things different?

What if you wore some funny glasses today
and pretended they had magical powers in some way?

What will you be capable of achieving?
how will your day shift and stop your grieving?

Stop thinking so much and go on a journey of fun
imagine all you do is run. . .

For no other reason that you want to
imagine this and know it's true

Metamorphosis Of A Misfit

Seeing through a little ones eyes
seeing the world full of surprise

How will this be different from your usual view?
how will it feel to recharge and renew?

Anything's possible with curiosity, imagination and believe
release, drop it, stop the grief

If only for a moment
believe you are potent

On a whole new universe unimaginable
energy levels full

Every wish coming to life
releasing strife

Take a look through a childlike lens
watch grass grow and flying wrens

Why do we see so differently than we once did?
why do we feel the need to keep a lid. . .

On our enthusiasm, passion and celebration
life is just an awesome creation

We can create and recreate every day of our lives
cheering others on with high fives!

Metamorphosis Of A Misfit

Even if just for a moment in time
feel sweet sublime

Feel everything in multicolor beauty and sound
you've been found

By the inner YOU
who's always been in queue

Waiting for you to summon them to show you the way
to add more fun, lightness and possibility to your day

What lens do you choose to see life through
it's totally up to you

Make a choice and smile with satisfaction
knowing you've taken affirmative action

As little eyes don't see racism or hate
they're compassionate, kind, loving and first rate

Take a page from a kids book
take a deeper look

Get lost in a painting or chat with a stranger
pretending there is no danger

Time is short and so were you
tell me, what will you do?

Metamorphosis Of A Misfit

To honor your younger self
put them on the top shelf

I look forward to hearing your view
maybe a picture of a tutu!

Or some other fanciful affair
to allow stuffy people to stare

I dare you to allow someone to smile
go that extra mile

To sprinkle joy on this land
take someones hand

Make it a brighter place
in this human race

Metamorphosis Of A Misfit

Reflection Questions

1. What's the funnest thing you've done in your life?

2. What was something you loved doing as a little kid?

3. How will you add a little sparkle to your day? Even if it's wearing a phenomenal pair of sparkly undies that know one can see!

4. Who will benefit from you lightening up a little?
   _____
   _____
   _____
   _____
   _____
   _____
   _____

5. How will you add play time in your life, to let your younger self shine?
   _____
   _____
   _____
   _____
   _____
   _____
   _____

6. How will your day look different when viewing it through a childlike lens?
   _____
   _____
   _____
   _____
   _____
   _____
   _____

7. What would happen if you chatted with a young person and asked them to solve your complex adult problems? If nothing else, this is hilarious and if you don't have your own young kids, borrow someones to complete this assignment! If this feels too creepy then get a crayon or colored pen, put it in your non dominant hand and write a question with your regular hand in boring adult color, then answer the question immediately (without thinking, taping into your sub-conscious) with an awesome crayon or colored pen. This can provide surprising and amazing insights!

Imagine

This poem was inspired when I realized (AGAIN) that the advice I'd given a client was exactly what I needed to hear myself! My client had lost sight of the wonders and potential within her. She was stuck in a belief system that her life currently, would always be this way. She was depressed, frustrated and longed for her life to be in alignment with her incredible talents and gifts. I reflected on the mountains of self help books I'd read and one story stuck with me. The story of Viktor Frankl. This incredible man was an Austrian neurologist and psychiatrist. What's astounding about Viktor is the WAY he survived the Holocaust. Freedom of choice, was something he lived by and despite conditions, he found meaning out of suffering. Viktor turned tragedies into a personal triumph. He believed in the freedom to take a stand. Imagination is part of finding exquisite meaning in your life. "If you can imagine it, you can achieve it" said William Arthur Ward. Visualization techniques are powerful, and using these and imagination to shape the life you want, gets results. Sometimes, it's only in your imagination that you can you find freedom, in your life.

Metamorphosis Of A Misfit

Imagine there is no failure for you
imagine that whatever you do

You'll be lifted to higher heights
you may not see it now, there may be some fights

Imagine everything is in divine order in your life
there may be pleasures, there may be strife

Imagine you can do no wrong
you are blessed and sing like the most exquisite bird song

You can leap and fly
you don't need to understand why

Just imagine there's a higher force
something allowing you to believe in a magnificent course

Imagine you can let your worries go and feel free
can you imagine that with me?

All your past is exactly that
you get to recreate your future, wear a different hat

Imagine waking each morning, knowing you will create a new you
knowing this, what will you do?

Who will you be and how will you act
what will you strive for and make a pact

Metamorphosis Of A Misfit

What is it, that scares you most
traveling the world or living by the coast?

Whatever it may be
imagine you are free

Imagination is powerful and healing
it can be incredible and revealing

Imagine the you, 5 years from now
what do you look like, breath and allow

Do you take your breath away? Do you move with grace?
are you serene and can you see your face?

Maybe older, wiser and free
this is the way, you will be

Imagine the future you, your inner guide
what will you share with you and what will you hide?

Do you have questions from your heart
what difference do you see? What sets you apart?

You are the present, as well as the, future you
with your guidance and spirit, what will you do?

Imagine your ideal self, the best version of your potential
capturing your true power is essential

Metamorphosis Of A Misfit

Imagine you have an incredible unique skill set
imagine all your highest intentioned goals are met

Imagine you will or imagine you won't, think of the power
you can flourish and rejoice or cower

The choice is yours and imagination is key
to get you, to where you want to be

Remember when you were little and imagination seemed real
what if a part of it was, and that was the deal?

We know sport psychologists and coaches use it all the time
that's what motivates people to operate in their prime

Imagination is a succulent delight
it can launch you to take flight

Imagination can take you places you've never been
show you things, yet to be seen

Where will you go in imagination land
who will support you and take your hand

Let me guide you now to a beautiful place
the place of your dreams, take a look at your face

The face reflected back at you in 5 years' time
graceful and secure, it's you in your prime

Metamorphosis Of A Misfit

What will the 5 years in the future you, say?
what will that person reveal that'll make your day?

The deep care, respect and love you have for you
there is not a thing you wouldn't do

What question will you ask YOU to reveal?
what layers will you uncover when you start to peel

Layer after layer, what advice will you depart
what will you uncover, that'll touch your heart

Imagine you give yourself a divine gift
what will be inside, how will you shift?

Your life from a place of stuck to sublime
imagination is power and time

Why put off now what you can do tomorrow?
it's you dream or your sorrow

So imagine my friends and imagine now
think of the solutions and how

How you can master your greatest desire
what will allow you to go higher and higher

Imagine the solutions and answers you need
what for you is the magical seed?

Metamorphosis Of A Misfit

Imagine, imagine then experience the joy
of living your life with a fantastical ploy

If you can dream it you can achieve it, for real
that's one, mighty fine deal!

Imagine into a life you desire
feel at peace like an eagle flyer

Soar high
and know when you die. . .

You've lived a life worth living
a story worthy tale from an inspirational being

I know you have it in you, I see it clear
so trust your instincts, make friends with your fear

You can go any direction you choose
take action that'll lead you to phenomenal hues

Colors and goals, you never imagined possible, on this earth
your imagination, passion, inspiration is your net worth

Live a life that you're proud to live
be generous and often give

Spend time searching for your true gifts to share
you may live a life without a care

Metamorphosis Of A Misfit

You care about what matters most, release the rest
imagine stress as a leaving guest

Imagine my friend, what you'll experience and see
when you imagine life, the way you choose it to be

Reflection Questions

1. Where does your imagination take you?

2. When you were little, what did your imagination conjure up?

3. If imagination can cause relief from pain, what else is it capable of? How can imagination serve you in life?

_____

_____

4. If you imagine the future you, what; images, sounds, and feelings arise?

_____

_____

_____

_____

_____

_____

_____

_____

5. Imagine you're the best you possible, what's that version of you doing? How are you living your life? What do you look like?

_____

_____

_____

_____

_____

_____

_____

_____

6. Imagine you had a super power, unique to you, what is it? How will you utilize your super power?

_____

_____

_____

_____

7. Imagine the universe granting you, what you most authentically desired. How will your life be different with these desires fulfilled?

Illusion Of Limitation

This poem was inspired when I was starting my business and getting so confused with which direction to go in. There was a plethora of; advice, articles, videos, speakers, sages, PDF's, webinars, and training courses, my head was about to explode. I felt torn when people advised me to do things in a certain way and it just didn't feel like me. I felt like I needed to be a cardboard cut out of someone else who was successful. I felt my power being stripped away. I felt vulnerable, raw and uncomfortable. Becoming a replica of other people was exhausting and pulling me away from who I really wanted to be. I lost hope that I could 'be me' and be financially secure. I was tired, helpless and felt like giving up. Through a variety of occurrences, I realized, I had a choice! I could walk the walk of a recalibration specialist and change my belief system or I could live an unauthentic life and be miserable! I chose to walk the walk and although there have been many ups and downs over the years, never, have I regretted taking this path.

Metamorphosis Of A Misfit

What are your limitations?
are they real, perceived or passed on from relations?

I had limitations coming out the wazoo
could it be, you feel them too?

I thought and believed and told others they were real
that's just how I was, that's the deal

It didn't occur to me, I may have been wrong
this realization hit me like a gong!

Right in the face of my beliefs, value and life story
some I was not willing to part with, held on for life and glory

Not seeing, it was dulling my shine
not understanding the power to release them was mine

Mine alone, I had a choice
what would I tell myself and others, what's my true voice?

It took journeys and miles, souls and heartache
to get a clear direction, be true and not fake

I'd been living life with a mask
not letting anyone see this monumental task

I was shocked and hurt the day I realized I was not a perfect being!
goodness, it was also a relief and blessing

Metamorphosis Of A Misfit

Of course on some level, I'd always known
there was a trail of clues, my cover was blown!

When I consciously made a decision to live from the heart
take the road less travelled, stand apart. . .

That's when I felt my brilliance shine through
I felt warm and tingly, no longer blue

No doubt there were ups and downs
yet not as severe, no restrictive gowns

I felt a freedom, a glow
a sense that even though

I didn't have all the answers right now
it was ok and safe and to take a sensational vow

I'd experienced glimpses of this throughout my life
scattered and mingled with struggle and strife

Although the way ahead is not clearly known
I can recognize how much I've grown

It's sparkling clear
the path is near

The path that's heartfelt and centered
that place, I'm in my element, not like a space rented

Metamorphosis Of A Misfit

The joy, bliss and wholeness I feel
is not frivolous, it's a huge deal

Some cards dealt, may leave you feeling jaded
yet I realized they can be traded and upgraded!

Now I have choice, the power of no
the direction I travel, which way I'll go

I thrive with this releasing of what I'm capable of and what I'm not
the world's my oyster, a blank canvas is my lot

What colors will I wear, what textures, I desire
I spread my wings and fly above mountains and higher

The sky is the limit and beyond
now that I have the sacred bond

The bond between ego and spirit mind
just let go and see what you find

Limiting beliefs will limit your sight
as Henry said, "think you will or think you won't", either way you're right

Who will you become when your clipped wings are healed?
what'll lay in front of you, in the golden field?

Who will be inspired by your flight?
who'll be given the gift of sight?

Metamorphosis Of A Misfit

It's powerful to assist someone to see
like a caged bird, being set free

Release your limited beliefs to the wind
live free instead of pinned

Pinned to a life that's not yours
feeling life is ground hog day, just pause

Look around and within
choose a win-win

Shining bright
is your birthright

Take flight my friend and fly home
or travel the earth and roam

Either way, you'll see
the power of here and now, just be

Flexible in your thoughts and outcomes, take time to mend
who're you to know the future and what's around the bend?

Trust have faith, let go of perceived limits and ties
experience what it's like to live, without lies

Live in honesty, best you can
that'll make you an inspiring woman or man

Metamorphosis Of A Misfit

Beliefs are yours to create
imagine the life of your creation, now open the gate

The gateway to your true potential
this my friend, in a heartfelt life, is essential

Metamorphosis Of A Misfit

Reflection Questions

1. What limitations do you have?

   _____
   _____
   _____
   _____
   _____
   _____
   _____
   _____

2. What evidence do you have, that these limitations are real?

   _____
   _____
   _____
   _____
   _____
   _____
   _____
   _____

3. What are you capable of without these limitations?

   _____
   _____
   _____
   _____
   _____
   _____
   _____

4. When do you NOT feel like you have limitations? When do you feel most capable?

_____

_____

_____

_____

_____

_____

_____

_____

5. How will your life change when your limitations are shifted/lifted?

_____

_____

_____

_____

_____

_____

_____

_____

6. What's the COST to you, of holding tight to your limitations?

_____

_____

_____

_____

_____

_____

_____

_____

7. What does the future you, look and sound like? If the future you offered advice, to create your desired life, what would that be?

-Author Bio-

Kirsty inspires Misfit Leaders to: achieve the impossible through unimaginable innovations, turn road blocks into stepping stones, ignite massive impacts, communicate like ninjas, create empowerment empires, and turn mindsets into magnificent motivators! She's presented trainings and key notes for: BRAVA, Center for Exceptional Leadership, Dream Bank (American Family Insurance), Edgewood High School, Gilda's Club, Group Health Cooperative, National Kidney Foundation, Health Grades, TASK, United Cerebral Palsy Association, National Association of Social Workers, Wisconsin Association Of Volunteer Services, and Wisconsin Representatives Of Activity Professionals.

She has a Master's degree in Teaching, Bachelor of Social Science in Business and Tourism, she's a Neuro-Linguistic Programmer (NLP), Certified Life & Health Coach and a member of the National Speakers Association (NSA).

Kirsty has a unique blend of humor, education and diverse life experience, to make her trainings and key notes; educational, energetic, and engaging. She's traveled the world; Australia, New Zealand, Bolivia, Peru, Argentina, Singapore, Canada, Italy, Switzerland, Amsterdam, England, Thailand, and the USA. She's lived and worked in five different countries and currently resides in Wisconsin USA. In her spare time Kirsty; goes on outdoor adventures with her family and pets, dances with fire pois, writes books, takes photographs, creates sparkly outfits to wear, plays in the gym, and swings in her hammock.

Stay in touch with Kirsty at: www.aussiespeaker.com

www.ingramcontent.com/pod-product-compliance
Lightning Source LLC
Chambersburg PA
CBHW080329170426
43194CB00014B/2508